Family Violence

WOMEN FROM THE MARGINS

An Orbis Series Highlighting Women's Theological Voices

Women from the Margins introduces a series of books that present women's theological voices from around the world. As has long been recognized, women have shaped and continue to shape theology in distinctive ways that recognize both the particular challenges and the particular gifts that women bring to the world of theology and to ministry within the church. Their theological voices reflect the culture in which they live and the religious practices that permeate their lives.

Also in the Series:

Family Violence

Reclaiming a Theology of Nonviolence

Elizabeth Soto Albrecht

ORBIS BOOKS

Maryknoll, New York 10545

Founded in 1970, Orbis Books endeavors to publish works that enlighten the mind, nourish the spirit, and challenge the conscience. The publishing arm of the Maryknoll Fathers and Brothers, Orbis seeks to explore the global dimensions of the Christian faith and mission, to invite dialogue with diverse cultures and religious traditions, and to serve the cause of reconciliation and peace. The books published reflect the views of their authors and do not represent the official position of the Maryknoll Society. To learn more about Maryknoll and Orbis Books, please visit our website at www.maryknoll.org.

Published by Orbis Books, Maryknoll, New York 10545-0308.
Manufactured in the United States of America.
Manuscript editing and typesetting by Joan Weber Laflamme.

Library of Congress Cataloging-in-Publication Data

Albrecht, Elizabeth Soto.
    Family violence : reclaiming a theology of nonviolence / Elizabeth Soto Albrecht.
        p. cm. — (Women from the margins)
    Includes bibliographical references and index.
    ISBN 978–1–57075–757–0
    1. Church work with problem families. 2. Family violence—Religious aspects—Christianity. I. Title.
    BV4438.5.A43 2008
    261.8'327—dc22
                                                                        2007046266

In memory of Letty Russell, my dear professor,
for J. Shannon Clarkson,
and for my thesis adviser and friend, Ruth E. Krall;
they all believed in me.

And from the past,
my aunts Isabel Soto Fuentes and Celia Soto Matias
for their life stories that I hold sacred
and that give me the courage to work for justice and peace
for women suffering from violence.
In gratitude for all the women
who shared their stories in the formation of this book.

For the future,
the loves of my life, our two girls,
Yentli Elis and Sara Liliana.
I pray they will be equipped to confront violence
and bring healing to this world.

Contents

Introduction

A friend of mine, Linda Crockett,[1] has shared with many friends her personal account of family violence. A strong advocate of abused women and a provider of support for survivors of family violence at the Samaritan Counseling Center in Lancaster, Pennsylvania, Linda is a social-justice activist and community educator dedicated to healing the wounds of abuse. She frequently traveled to El Salvador during the 1980s to lead church delegations and accompany refugees struggling to survive in war zones, and her journeys put her in touch with the wounds of abuse in her own family. This is the story of her childhood and her reflection on it as she told it to me.

I was thirty-two years old when I first entered the war zones of Central America, but I grew up in a war zone in a rural community in Lancaster County, Pennsylvania. The neat brick walls of the house my father built belied the violence committed within, hiding it from the eyes of the casual passerby.

The term "battered-child syndrome" was coined in 1961 (I was only six) from a growing awareness of the need to protect children from physical abuse. My father, upset by this, muttered that the government had no right to interfere with the family. His admonition that "what goes on in this house stays in this house" was repeated so often that it became our family mantra.

There is nothing worse than suffering alone, believing yourself to be abandoned by the world. The child I was knew this after suffering alone for years. And it wasn't until my time in El Salvador that I began my journey of resurrection.

I had moved through early adulthood in a fog with little memory of major family events. Emotionally numb, I felt compelled at times to hurt myself in secret. I had pushed away the

1

memory of my mother's abuse, which had intricately linked sexual pleasure and pain. While we usually think of men as the primary abusers, women can, and do, sexually and physically abuse not only their sons, but also their daughters.

In 1992, I made a decision to seek healing through therapy. I confronted my father with the fact that I had been abused and the life-long consequences of his refusal to protect me. I began by telling him how painful his abandonment of me was at age five after being molested by my teenage cousin and his friends. I reminded him that he had witnessed my mother physically abusing me many times. When I demanded to know why he had not stopped her, he admitted she was "too hard" on me and said that he talked to her privately about it. I asked him what her response was. "She told me to go to hell, and to mind my own damn business." He shrugged, as if to say he had no recourse.

I began to cry. I asked him how he could let her hurt me like that. "I thought she was a good mother," he said. It was his response to almost every incident of abuse I recounted that day.

It is unfortunate that survivors sometimes feel pressured by church teachings to forgive their abusers and those who stood by silently. Forgiveness has its place in the healing process for some survivors. However, it should never be imposed or presented as the ultimate goal of healing.

It took two years of therapy to reclaim my tears. They had been forbidden by my mother even as she inflicted unspeakable pain on my body. It took six years to begin to feel my anger, which was an equally essential part of my healing. Directing my rage toward those who had hurt me liberated my anger, allowing it to become a force to empower me to speak for those who continue to suffer in silence.

Religion and faith can be a resource or a roadblock for survivors. The religion of my parents served to oppress the vulnerable and legitimate the violence of those in authority. The ideology of submission and obedience reinforced the belief that whatever God—or parents—did was always "for our own good." When I was a child, my pastor ignored obvious signs of distress in our family and even defended my parents against a doctor's accusations of abuse.

Family violence is the proverbial elephant in the living room around which we stumble but largely refuse to acknowledge. Too often, the cries of the victims are heard only by God. It's time for us to change that.[2]

THE ALARMING REALITY

Linda's story points to the alarming fact that this social disease called family violence is rampant and widespread, affecting all classes and ethnicities. A survivor of sexual abuse once told me, "Abuse is so prevalent for women that it is no longer a question of who will be abused but a matter of when." Victims and survivors are everywhere, hidden by the walls of their houses and even sitting in church pews. Family violence exists all over the world, although it manifests itself quite differently in the world's many cultures. Globally, at least one woman in every three will be beaten, coerced into sex, or abused in her lifetime.[3] Family violence is typically gender-based violence, because we live in a patriarchal society that treats women as inferior human beings, which is reflected in the daily interactions within families. Family violence is recognized today as both a major health concern and a violation of human rights.[4] Any form of violence is also a serious religious problem.

Reports on family violence in the United States, according to the Department of Justice Family Violence Statistics Report of June 2005, provide statistics for the year 2000 from the National Incident-Based Reporting System. This means data is gathered only when an incident is reported to the police, so the statistics may not reflect the true reality lived by many U.S. citizens. For each incident reported, two more may go unreported by family members simply because "this is a private matter." The Justice Department reports that between 1998 and 2002 "of these roughly 3.5 million violent crimes committed against family members, 49% were crimes against spouses, 11% were sons or daughters victimized by a parent, and 41% were crimes against other family members." The most frequent type of family violence was simple assault. Also, about three-fourths of all family violence occurred in or near the victim's residence. The majority (73 percent) of victims were female, most family violence offenders were white (79 percent), and most offenders were thirty or older (62 percent).[5]

Over the last ten years Latino families have suffered an alarming increase in violence in the home. In Puerto Rico, for example, every week and a half a woman is killed at the hands of her spouse or ex-husband.[6] In Colombia records of a governmental agency for the protection of women indicate that in 2002 a woman was battered as a victim of domestic violence every twelve minutes.[7] In Honduras in 1999 the Pan-American Health Organization registered the deaths of eight women per month at the hands of their husbands or ex-husbands.[8] The forms of violence carried out within the family space when parents cannot manage conflict nonviolently result in both physical harm, sometimes even in death, and often long-lasting emotional scars.

The story of the social disease of family violence can be traced back through the centuries. "Herstory," including the stories of wives, mothers, daughters, and widows, has often gone untold, undocumented, and unnamed—from the horrifying story of abuse suffered by the Levite's concubine in Judges 19 to the African women of the seventeenth century who were captured for the colonizers of the "New World." Taken by force by both African and European men and purchased by rich white male landowners throughout South America, the Caribbean, and North America, these girls and women were regarded as property to be used for labor and to satisfy sexual appetites. Also included in "herstory" are the countless indigenous women who were forced to procreate illegitimate children for the colonizers. The African women (and men) and the indigenous populations of the world were objects to be used and abused by the patriarchal mentality of that time, a mentality that still is present today.

Family violence is a deeply felt women's issue, but it is not just a women's issue. It should be an issue for all people, including men, and for all religious bodies, and for all organizations seeking the common good. Closely related to patriarchy are contemporary social issues such as continuing violence against women and children, poverty, and health issues such as HIV/AIDS. Across the beautiful landscapes of Africa live women afflicted by HIV/AIDS; many are faithful married women who have been exposed to the virus by their unfaithful husbands. The same is true in Latin America and Asia, where patriarchal systems commonly permit men to have multiple sexual partners. Thus HIV/AIDS, another form of violence committed against women and innocent children, spreads at an alarming rate. In patriarchal systems, as Sophia Chirongoma reminds us in an article on women, poverty, and HIV in Zimbabwe, "although women are responsible for most of the production and processing of the food crops, men control the means of production, land, cattle and reproduction."[9]

In Japan, Hisako Kinukawa, a leading Japanese feminist theologian and biblical scholar, has written of another patriarchal system that the Japanese government tried to hide from view since World War II: after the invasion of Korea by Japan, girls and women were lured to Japan with the promise of job opportunities only to wake up as "comfort women," sex slaves for the Japanese soldiers. The same was true in the Philippines. Today these women cry for justice by sharing their stories in the hope of public recognition of the wrong done to them. They were victims of racism, sexism, militarism, imperialism, and colonialism.[10] These patriarchal systems, "legitimized" in many ways, sometimes even by religious belief, are yet another form of violence toward women. Even today women and girls around the world, usually because of poverty, are offered "contracts" to work in more developed countries as domestic workers, waitresses, and models, yet once they arrive they are forced to work as sex entertainers or prostitutes.

In *Korean Women and God* theologian Choi Hee An highlights how women are strongly influenced by traditional religious beliefs, including Christianity, that define and limit their roles and thus their lives. When Korean women are expected to be good wives, sacrificing mothers, and modest daughters and daughter-in-laws, women can become no more than instruments of the success of men. Choi also notes that Korean women are still used as a source of cheap labor and are expected to generate additional income for their families.[11]

The United States is no exception. *A Troubling in My Soul: Womanist Perspectives on Evil and Suffering*, edited by Emilie M. Townes, contains a series of illuminating essays that describe the experiences of African American women from the narratives of slaves to the present.[12] The writings of Ada María Isasi-Díaz and other Hispanic/Latina scholars describe the experiences of immigrant women from Latin America.[13] We also have the memoirs of Abigail Abbot Bailey published in 1815. Mrs. Bailey, an eighteenth-century churchwoman from New England, was abused by her husband, who committed adultery with their female servants and incest with his seventeen-year-old daughter. Mrs. Bailey described her experience in abundant detail. As noted above, today in this country one in three women will be affected by domestic violence during her lifetime, and each year 5.3 million additional women become victims in the United States.

MY SOCIAL CONTEXT

My life experiences, starting in Puerto Rico, my country of birth, bring together several Latino cultures. I have also lived among Latinos/ Latinas in the United States, have served seven years in mission work in Colombia, and have traveled extensively throughout Central and South America. Born in a Puerto Rican Catholic family, I chose in my teens to join the Mennonite Church in Arecibo, Puerto Rico. I became actively involved in that small mission church, and in order to better serve my people, I decided to study theology after completing a bachelor's degree in health education from the University of Puerto Rico. I then started a master's degree in theology at the Seminario Evangelico de Puerto Rico in 1982. In 1984 I completed my studies at the Associate Mennonite Biblical Seminary in Elkhart, Indiana, under the sponsorship and generosity of the Mennonite churches in Puerto Rico. My desire was to study Anabaptist history and theology to deepen my understanding and own the theological teaching of my church in order to better serve its gospel of peace.

After finishing seminary and during my work at a local Mennonite agency, I received training to become a volunteer at the local YWCA in Elkhart, Indiana, trying to help women victims of domestic violence who sought a way out. I was particularly interested in being available for Latina victims. Later, when I was teaching Bible classes at a local college, I began walking the streets of some small Midwestern towns to work with white middle-class women (discovering that violence wasn't limited to immigrants!) and to take them to a hospital and then a secret shelter. The numbers astonished me. After completing a doctorate in ministry at San Francisco Theological Seminary, I knew I had found my life's work.

As I continue to assist white, black, and Latina women, I remember clearly the story of my aunt Celia, a story that was being lived over and over by so many women and their innocent children. My family helped my aunt escape from a violent husband late one night, and even today I carry her desperate cry for help inside me as I help total strangers. As a Christian, a church leader, a theologian, and a feminist I have looked to my church many times and asked how it could help victims of family violence. Sadly, many women victims have given up on the church because the church often sends them back home, telling them to pray until the problem goes away. Today, the church has become more aware of the problem, but it still has a long way to go. While we have stronger laws and more effective health and social services for victims, family violence shows no sign of abating. In the end, this project was conceived in the tears of victims and the enlightenment of the women and men who were searching to be church to these victims.

THE MENNONITE THEOLOGY OF NONVIOLENCE

As a Mennonite, I write from within my tradition. Upheld as a doctrinal principle by the Anabaptists[14] and Mennonites and based on the gospel of peace, the theology of nonviolence has been applied primarily to issues of war and injustice in local and international settings. These biblical teachings have not really been drawn upon to bring peace to the family. Yet, it seems to me, this theology of nonviolence is foundational to the well-being of families, particularly those families hovering on the precipice of violence, and it can help promote healing in families that have already experienced family violence.

By building on the image of Christ, the maker of peace, I hope to provide tools to help overcome family violence in North America. Families caught in cycles of violence need much guidance to return to the peace principles of Jesus and to learn peace skills[15] that can help them improve their quality of life. As a feminist studying the theology of nonviolence, I examine practical ways these biblical and theological principles can be used to overcome family violence with the goal of bringing peace into Christian homes.

I believe that the church, the body of Christ, is called to be present when members become aware of family violence. The church can also be instrumental in encouraging the development of laws that will do more to bring about justice and to assure the protection of victims and their children. Given the degree of trauma and poverty that affect people today, churches must do more than simply focus on legal matters. Churches must channel their efforts where they are most needed and refer people in need to the legal, psychological, and social resources available where they live. As Christians, our task should be to accompany these victims on their journey to healing. Christians have much to offer, particularly if they make better use of biblical resources and the richness of Christian spirituality to contribute to the process of healing.

As Christians, how can we call attention to the violent behaviors and unhealthy patterns present in our communities, and how can we walk with people in order to help families? What can a church with a theology of nonviolence do to help them? How can a theology of nonviolence be used to overcome family violence? What are the needs of individuals and families who experience explosions of gender-based abuse of power and repressive, overt, and covert violence in the home?

FAMILY VIOLENCE–THE IMAGE OF A TREE

In counseling families I often work with the image of a tree, and this is how I've chosen to organize this book. Chapter 1, "Examining the Leaves," begins with the leaves of the tree. The first thing we usually notice about a tree is its leaves; similarly, the first indications of the presence of violence within a family are the scars, both physical and emotional, left behind. In this chapter I describe the presence of family violence, its forms, manifestations, and significance for families and churches.

In the second chapter, "Branches That Connect," I turn to the branches that support the leaves, attempting to uncover and explain some of the significant factors—cultural, social, and economic—that lead to family violence. By using the approach of social analysis, I examine in greater detail the cultural, social, economic, and emotional or psychological factors that produce violence within families.

When a tree is heavy with branches and leaves, the trunk is often hidden. Think in particular of an evergreen tree or a willow tree. In Chapter 3, "Nutrients within the Trunk," I move in closer to examine the trunk, and I turn to the Mennonite tradition of a theology of nonviolence. The tradition, reclaimed and interpreted through a feminist lens, can supply valuable nutrients to nourish the tree and move it from violence to peace.

In Chapter 4, "Exposing the Roots," I explore how the roots of the family tree can be poisoned, for example, by silence and by "normalizing" violence, and also how these roots can receive proper nutrients to nourish peace. The final chapter, "Peace That Brings Healing," focuses on the desired outcome—how churches can accompany families on their journey to healing and create a culture of peace. The colorful fabric of North America is woven of many cultures and subcultures in which the disease of family violence is present. I maintain that churches must play a vital role in replacing violence with peace. This is the path for followers of Jesus, the peacemaker par excellence.

Recently my family and I won a "free" get-away to a large time-share resort on the East Coast. After we completed the required ninety-minute tour and sales pitch (altogether nearly three hours), the sales representative, an elegant blonde, middle-aged woman with a strong southern accent, shared her sad story of abuse. I was in the middle seat of our minivan trying to entertain our two daughters and two college friends during this already overextended tour of the resort grounds, but I overheard her telling my husband about the abuse she endured at home.

At first I wondered why she was sharing such a personal story with us. We were total strangers. Then I felt overwhelmed and powerless to help her, and I wondered if God felt I should be "on duty" that day, even though I was on vacation. Did I need to be working? I work with troubled families. This polite, well-groomed woman had just ended a twenty-five-year-old marriage because her husband was emotionally and physically abusive. She knew she deserved a better life, and she broke the cycle of that violent life by removing herself from it. She had taken the first step. Like many middle-class women who suffer from abusive relationships, she also suffered by ending the relationship. Her lifestyle and all her supports fell apart, and all she could anticipate was misery. The economic impact of the breakup of a marriage is much harder on women than on men. In addition, many have often struggled for years to keep their families together, which makes it even harder to leave the abusive home.

The thought crossed my mind that perhaps sharing her sad story was a ploy to get us to buy into the time-share in order to help her out. I felt sympathy for her, but I did not want to be manipulated into buying something that we could not afford and that conflicts with the simple lifestyle we have chosen. (Even if we did have the extra money, we could put it to far better use helping people who really must struggle to live.) Although we turned down her sales pitch, we felt the need to provide her with some encouragement because as a family we have made a commitment to carry the message of God's love to this hurting world.

Instead of a commission, we wanted to give a "God gift." As we said goodbye, we thanked the saleswoman for treating us in such a gentle, gracious manner. She responded that her prayers were that she would find someone who would really love her because she felt she had never received love during her twenty-five years of marriage. I silently mourned that most women are socialized to believe that complete happiness can be achieved only by finding a man to love us. This is part of the patriarchal mentality embedded in women from the time they are young and also a major root of the problems, including abuse, that women endure throughout their lives. Silently, I prayed that she would not fall into another abusive relationship because of her emotional need to feel loved and that she could learn first to love herself and the life without violence that she had chosen.

My prayer is that this book might help at least one family, one victim, or one young girl overcome family violence; this alone will justify the many hours I've spent counseling, researching, and writing. I hope as well that it might motivate church leaders to become more informed and involved in overcoming family violence. It really does take a community to overcome violence and build a culture of peace. And should it not be led by the community of the followers of Jesus, who taught us about nonviolence as the pathway to peace?

1

Examining the Leaves

Naming the Problem

The leaves of the many species of trees throughout the world come in a variety of sizes and shapes because they have adapted to their different environments. Family violence, a global problem that is present in most countries and that affects a large segment of people, also takes many forms and corresponds to its environment. The ground that is most fertile for family violence seems to be an environment permeated with the belief that men must be in control, that women have only a reproductive role, that children are owned and valued as possessions, and that the elderly and disabled are disposable human beings. These signs of inequality for the more vulnerable members of society are also indicators of the potential for family violence. In our approach to family violence we need to begin by studying the "leaves," the outward signs of the presence of violence, to get a clear grasp of the challenges we face.

The most visible signs of family violence are the physical and emotional scars that result. While verbal abuse does not leave physical scars, its power should not be underestimated, because verbal abuse and emotional abuse have hidden but long-term effects on the victims. The childhood playground chant of "sticks and stones may hurt my bones, but words will never hurt me" is more realistically rendered as "sticks and stones may bruise my skin, but words will hurt forever." It is important to emphasize that family violence produces emotional baggage that will burden its victims throughout their entire lives.

Statistics today show that every fifteen seconds in the United States a woman is beaten; two out of every five women who are murdered are killed by their husbands. Eighty-five percent of all cases of abuse involve men beating women; of the 15 percent of men who are abused, 7 percent are abused by their male partners. Domestic violence takes place in all cultures, religions, and classes; no family is exempt from its threat—and this includes Christian families. In addition, it is important to note that violence in the home usually becomes more frequent and severe over time. It is not surprising that children who grow up in violent homes come to believe that violence is normal and also an acceptable way to control others.

Sexual abuse is one of the most devastating types of violence a person can experience. For a woman it represents an injury and a brokenness to the most intimate part of who she is. A woman's sexuality is shattered in pieces, and it may take a lifetime to patch it together again. The terrible possibility that the abuse may recur hovers grimly throughout her life.

The World Health Organization (WHO) defines sexual abuse as "any sexual act, attempt to obtain a sexual act, unwanted sexual comments or advances, or acts to traffic, or otherwise directed against a person's sexuality using coercion, by any person regardless of their relationship to the victim, in any setting, including but not limited to home and work."[1] Sexual abuse takes many forms, including rape, date rape, nonconsensual intercourse, sexual abuse of children, forced marriage, denial of one's right to use contraception, forced abortion, female genital mutilation, and obligatory inspections for virginity. The seduction of women and girls when vulnerable is also termed abuse. During their lifetimes, as many studies show, one out of three women will experience sexual violence in one or another of these forms. Unfortunately, throughout history sexual abuse in this form has also been used as a weapon of war.

Male victims of sexual abuse are less likely to report such offenses because of the shame attached, but this does not mean that this type of abuse is not real. In most cultures men are socialized not to demonstrate "weaknesses" such as crying and not to talk openly about their feelings. This is also a form of oppression that is characteristic of patriarchal cultures. Fortunately, some specialized agencies exist that are geared to these concerns.

Abuse also exists within religion. While this form of abuse is more difficult to identify, it is a powerful force in many Christian homes and churches. In the name of the cross, many women are abused, tortured, and even killed to satisfy the common good of a male-oriented religion. In churches and in the media, sermons still promote the submission of women to men as part of the order established by God at creation. Advocates often use and abuse scripture to support their cause of "putting women in their place."

A more subtle form of abuse occurs when women's voices are removed from the decision-making processes in churches or when churches refuse to ordain women into ministry or to appoint them as supervisors or overseers. Although these issues have been resolved for many mainline Protestant denominations, even today some churches do not allow women to preach. This includes the more conservative Christian evangelical churches as well as the Roman Catholic Church. Marie Fortune reminds us that "the familial model of church life has developed in recent years in an effort to overcome the isolation of contemporary life and to build intimate, caring relationships among church members. Unfortunately, just as there is potential for abuse in families, there is potential for abuse in the church that views itself as family."[2]

It is also important to point out that family violence in most cases is gender-based violence that involves the physical, sexual, psychological, and economic abuse of girls and women. Gender-based violence has evolved in part from the subordinate status of women in society. Indeed, many cultures have beliefs, norms, and social institutions that legitimize and perpetuate violence against women. Acts that would be punished almost universally if directed at an employer or employee, a neighbor, or an acquaintance often go unchallenged when men direct them at women within family settings.[3]

According to the manual *No to Violence*[4] the term *abuse* suggests to some people that the behavior is more serious than the term *violence* would suggest. Others, however, regard *abuse* as less serious and even object to its use on the grounds that it minimizes the seriousness of violent behavior. As a result, the group No To Violence chooses to use the term *violence* to cover *all* behavior people regard as either violent or abusive and behavior that violates the right of another person to safety and well-being. Several programs aimed at changing men's behavior also address controlling patterns of behavior that display power over women and children. Family violence, therefore can include several forms of unacceptable social behavior, including actual abuse—physical, verbal, and emotional—as well as unjust controlling behavior.

The No To Violence group also points out that experts in the field do not necessarily agree on the terminology used. No To Violence discourages use of the terms *victims* or *survivors* for the more challenging language of "women and children who have experienced violence" or "those who have been violated." However, there is solid and widespread agreement that family violence does exist and that it damages people, destroying their human dignity and leaving them with ugly emotional and physical scars. Acknowledging that people are getting hurt in their homes by their loved ones is a good starting point.

GUIDING QUESTIONS

As a feminist, quite aware of the influence that my social context has on me, I have chosen to work on the complex issue of family violence. In doing so, I am in no way moving away from denouncing violence against women, but rather recognizing it as a manifestation of gender-based violence in our society and in families. Family is very dear to women's hearts, and whether the family is dysfunctional or healthy, it is honored. Women are socialized to protect the family, no matter what happens within the confines of our homes. I realize increasingly that women need to be treated within their family system whenever possible; it is a disservice to treat a woman without helping the entire family, if that is feasible. Healing several individuals in the unit is more life-giving and provides greater assurance that any positive changes brought about will endure.

Counseling victims of abuse requires much patience and much caution. Whatever we do, we must not cause more harm for the victims. It is essential to listen carefully to the victims and to trust the honesty of their statements in order to accompany them in their family situation. They know better than we what is safe for them and their children and, most of all, how we can assist them at the moment. Such an empowerment model is a preferred form of intervention with battered women.

One critical question that guides my work is why intra-family violence is present in Christian homes. This includes a set of parallel questions as well: Does our current peace theology contribute in any way to intra-family violence? Does the church ever act as an accomplice to a perpetrator? What happens when a church turns a blind eye and deaf ear to family violence by not believing, not knowing, not intervening? Without necessarily doing a statistical study, there is also a need to ask exactly who are the families or individuals who experience intra-family violence. Why are they suffering this evil alone? Are they aware of church teachings on a theology of *shalom*, peace, and nonviolence?

This book is intended to challenge all churches in the United States, particularly those that embrace a theology of nonviolence but have been slow to express their disapproval of family violence or to extend support to its victims. Many churches have spoken out courageously against the violence of war but not against violence in homes.[5] We need to ask the simple yet profound question of why this is so. Since a theology of peace was developed as a response to a context of war, can this same theology be used to resist the "wars" in homes? Or do feminists (women and men) need to create a new theology to respond to the needs of those who suffer violence within the walls of their homes?

NONVIOLENCE AS A TOOL

Anabaptism has a rich tradition with Jesus as a model for building peace. The Anabaptist movement started in the sixteenth century when its adherents resisted governmental and religious rules that went against the principal values of the "kin-dom"[6] of God. The kin-dom of God, where no one is excluded, is a nonhierarchical gathering of God and God's people.[7] However, sometime along the way it became easier to advocate for justice for the poor and ignore the cries of women. If a theology of peace does not advocate for the safety of Christian women who experience violence within supposedly Christian homes, it needs a closer look, and we must consider revising its vision and its programs. There are churches today that have achieved a degree of awareness and speak out against violence in the family. But how can these churches work for healing within families? As part of a peace theology, how can they lead men—fathers and husbands—into paths that are less macho, less in step with a sexist culture? How can churches take up the role of healer in the name of the Lord, the maker of peace? And most important of all, how can churches prevent violence in the family from occurring in the first place?

Peace communities have made few attempts to create alternatives to violence in the most basic social institution of the family. Anabaptist feminist theologians are currently working to identify some of the underlying beliefs within Christianity and Mennonite peace theology that contribute to the problem of gender-based violence. On the other hand, these beliefs can also prevent us from seeing and understanding the problem of violence in interpersonal relationships.[8] During the last two decades in Mennonite communities in North America, several courageous Mennonite feminists have begun to expose the painful reality that many church members—women, children, and men—have been living with violence in their Christian homes, some as victims of child sexual abuse and others as battered wives. The sexual misconduct of well-known Mennonite theologian John H. Yoder, which was exposed in the mid 1990s, is not an isolated example.[9]

Feeling disappointed by the church and its hierarchical system that protects abusers and underestimates the pain of the victims, I have attempted to expose these violent sins. Although I refer to the Mennonites (the group most familiar to me), I intentionally want to include all Christian churches. My goal is to call all Christian churches to examine once again what we are doing and how we are assisting the victims and their children who are worshiping in our churches.

The frustrating experiences of taking a woman beaten by her husband to the emergency room and taking others to a women's shelter only to have these women return home to their abusive husbands have encouraged me to imagine other options. I aim to empower abused women not to allow themselves to be beaten over and over again. However, because as human beings they have the option of choosing their own path in life, I must also respect their desire to stay in their homes even though the abuse may continue. My work takes me into many Christian homes. I always encourage victims to have a plan of safety in case the abuse should recur. In addition, I offer specific help if and when it seems needed. Occasionally I request, on behalf of the church, to work directly with the family to help them end the violence.

We need to highlight the role we believe the church has played or plays in perpetuating a theology that has been oppressive rather than liberating for women and families. Through its lack of involvement in family violence, churches have become accomplices, often protecting the male image and further victimizing women and children. There can be no neutral position when dealing with this issue. Breaking the cycle of violence must become a priority within all churches because Christ, the maker of peace, showed humankind a new way of being in the world, that of "active nonviolent resistance."[10]

DEFINITIONS AND CONCEPTS:
VIOLENCE AND *NONVIOLENCE*

Because *violence* and *abuse* can be interpreted in many ways, I want to be intentional about the terminology I am using; precise definitions are essential in establishing a framework to improve the life of families. Most important is the term *violence*. According to the *Dictionary of Feminist Theologies*, "the term *violence* may be applied equally to overt physical force or to covert structures of repression. What is common to both understandings, overt and covert violence, is *compulsion*."[11] Violence in this sense includes hidden or covert violence that does not necessarily do direct physical harm but nonetheless destroys human dignity. Dr. Ruth Krall refers to this as "a violation of personhood."[12] It is the subtle, institutionalized destruction of human possibilities that is around us all the time, although it may not be apparent to those who are comfortably situated. It is present, nonetheless, whenever the structures of society act to depersonalize human beings, and we need to be aware that our social and political systems can actually embed violence. In *The Verbally Abusive Relationship*, Patricia Evans notes a highly significant point: "Repressive systems perpetuate themselves as long as they remain unrecognized."[13]

Dom Hélder Câmara, a Brazilian priest who was the archbishop of Olinda and Recife in northeast Brazil and author of *Spiral of Violence* (1971), made a marvelous contribution to the world on the challenging theme of violence. In the middle of the 1970s unrest in Brazil, the largest country in Latin America, Dom Hélder had the courage to ask, Can nonviolent action serve the country?[14] Dom Hélder wrote to convince humankind of the absurdity of war; today, family violence should be challenged with the same degree of power.

Dom Hélder states clearly that violence is a challenge: "Violence is not the real answer to violence; if violence is met by violence, the world will fall into a spiral of violence; the only true answer to violence is to have the courage to face the injustices which constitute violence."[15] In order to arrive at peace, we must first do justice. In the words of Dom Hélder, "Justice is the condition for peace, the path, the way," and "injustice *is* violence.[16] Injustice is the root cause of violence, and one expression of such injustice is the abuse of power by men to control women.

The word *conflict* comes from the Latin *fligere*, meaning "to strike" or "to have friction between two people." Conflict does not necessarily equal violence. Conflict-management experts point out that conflict is a normal part of life and that social beings who live in family structures and interact with other family members will naturally experience conflict. The key to whether the conflict is violent or not lies in how we deal with these tensions and frictions. When conflict builds up between people and no resolution is sought or found by those affected by it, conflict can explode into violence.

Widely known international mediator John Paul Lederach explained in *Enredos, pleitos y problemas* (tangles, disputes, and problems) that "conflict is natural and necessary for growth and social transformation. We are not condemned to express our differences in inhumane ways."[17] The growth to which he refers is the opportunity to identify a problem and search for creative ways to solve differences. It is important, therefore, to equip family members to mediate their own problems before these problems turn into violent behavior. In particular, families with a history of violence need to learn how to break and then to keep from repeating patterns of violence.

The term *nonviolence* is preferred to *pacifism*. Throughout recent history the traditional peace churches have moved toward use of the term *nonviolence*. *Nonviolence* is understood as a method used by Christian pacifists to make peace; it is a lifestyle that attempts to eliminate violence, denounce injustice, and search for alternative ways of transforming conflict. It is a way of life aimed at negotiating, mediating, and/or reconciling, while respecting life and seeing the sacred in all the human beings of God's creation.

It is not surprising that *nonviolence* means different things to different people. Some mainstream Protestant church members criticize nonviolence as an ineffective means of bringing about change; they see it as too passive. At times the traditional peace churches, including among others the Mennonites, the Quakers, and members of the Church of the Brethren, have been ridiculed for their positions on peace issues. Nonetheless, members of these peace churches have chosen nonviolence as a way of life, with Jesus as their role model. As John Dear points out, Jesus frequently engaged in nonviolent activities and upheld the equality of all human beings, insisting that every human being is a daughter or a son of God.[18] Members of the peace churches believe that nonviolence is the only way to denounce the evil committed against life itself. Their active nonviolence is spiritually grounded, and it is the source of pacifist actions directed toward overcoming the violence that surrounds everyone today. They also maintain that violence tempts people to respond in the same violent way. Nonviolence consists in acting toward another person in the spirit of justice. Therefore, if violence is the absence of justice, then nonviolence can be a precondition for the possibility of justice.[19]

It is important to note that nonviolence has several different dimensions. *Principled nonviolence* is following Jesus regardless of personal cost. This is the nonviolence of faithfulness that is behind the stance of the Mennonite Church USA in not supporting war.

There is also *strategic nonviolence*, which describes the way we *do* nonviolence. This is the strategy used by the powerless in situations of overwhelming coercion. In many ways this is a response of women in situations of family violence. A prime example is demonstrated regularly by mothers who gather with other women in the Plaza de Mayo in Argentina on the same day of each week to cry for their disappeared loved ones. During the war in El Salvador in the 1980s, the *comadres* in El Salvador denounced to their government the injustice of the innocent being killed day after day. In *Power of the Weak* Elizabeth Janeway offers an additional example of this method of nonviolence, describing how victims actively set about disbelieving the lies of the victimizers and come together to empower each other for positive change.[20]

In *Reweaving the Web of Life*, feminist Pam McAllister, a longtime activist on peace and justice issues, compares what feminism and nonviolence have in common. She concludes, "Both oppose power that is exploitative and manipulative."[21] For many of us, nonviolence is an extension of feminism as we aim to dismantle the mental weaponry of a misogynist society. Nonviolence urges us never to hurt or kill one another, never to wage war, never to oppress others, never to do anything that would threaten the human race. We see it as necessary to integrate pacifism and feminism, although these two movements have not coincided throughout history. Christian feminism in general calls for a transformation of patriarchy, including male domination within the church, so we can live as the creation of God, women and men living together and working in justice and peace.[22]

Nonviolent conduct is the act of refraining from violence even under direct provocation or attack. This does not mean, however, that when a man hits a woman she should receive the beating passively. The abused person can choose a response that will reflect a nonviolent action. The woman may choose to address the abuser verbally, requesting that the abuse stop. She can denounce what she knows is wrong and tell the man why his actions are abusive to her. She may choose to leave the place of violence, and she may invoke her right to press charges. She may decide not to hit back or not to provoke him verbally and simply walk out. If the abuse ends, she may prepare a safe plan of escape in case the abuse begins again. All of these are concrete actions a woman can take that do not involve violence. It goes without saying that these actions require a degree of self-awareness of the situation and a firm decision to make better choices for herself and her children.

DEFINITION OF FAMILY VIOLENCE

A report prepared by the Office of Justice Program of the U.S. Department of Justice in June 2005 provided a legal definition of family violence: "Family Violence includes all types of violent crime committed by an offender who is related to the victim either biologically or legally through marriage or adoption. The crime [may be] done by a current or former spouse, parent or adoptive parents, current or former stepparents, [or] legal guardian."[23] It is easy to use the term *domestic violence* interchangeably with *family violence*, but family violence includes domestic violence as well as child abuse and elder abuse. Although they are used interchangeably, I prefer the term *family violence* because it is more inclusive. Because such forms of violence occur as a result of imbalanced power between males and females, violence in the family can also result in abusive child rearing, starting a cycle of violence that reproduces itself.

Leading experts on family violence do not always agree on definitions or possible actions to be taken. The issues involved in family violence are complex; there is no "simple truth" and therefore no easy solution.[24] Similarly, there is no common understanding of what a healthy family looks like and whether the focus should be on the entire family or only on the victims of violence. Many moral issues as well as social and economic issues play a part in family violence. When the interplay of such issues erupts in violence, stilling the conflict becomes both urgent and emotionally charged. This makes it extremely difficult to deal with family violence as research to be undertaken in logical and objective ways. However we choose to deal with such violence, we need to recognize it is a topic of study with practical, emotional, political, and moral dimensions. This is pointed out eloquently by Richard J. Gelles and Donileen Loseke in *Current Controversies on Family Violence*. It is generally agreed that it is a topic of public concern that needs to be addressed on many fronts: political, social, economic, and religious.

Two leading organizations in the Chicago area, Rainbow House and Mujeres Latinas en Accion, a U.S.-based Latina women's group that documents domestic violence and attempts to increase public awareness of the problem, define domestic violence as a "pattern of physical or psychological abuse, threats, intimidation, isolation or economic coercion used by one person to exert power and control over another person in the context of dating, family or household relationship."[25] Domestic violence is maintained by societal and cultural attitudes, institutions and laws, which are not consistent in naming this violence as wrong.

THE LEAVES: FORMS OF FAMILY VIOLENCE

Family violence can assume a number of forms, as shown below. This list is not exhaustive, and it should be noted that behaviors can fall into more than one category. Among the many definitions and types of family violence that are used, I have chosen these definitions from No To Violence[26] because they are *behavior-based* definitions that offer a larger range of manifestations of violence than many other definitions:

1. Emotional violence and controlling behaviour . . . does not accord equal importance and respect to another person's feelings and experiences. It is often the most difficult to pinpoint or identify. It can also be seen to underlie all of the other forms of violent and controlling behaviour. It includes the refusal to listen to or denial of the other's feelings, telling people what they do or do not feel and ridicule or shaming of the other's feelings. It also includes making the other responsible for one's own feelings, blaming or punishing them for how one feels, and manipulation by appeal to their feelings such as guilt, shame and worthlessness. It also includes emotional control such as telling someone directly or indirectly

that if she expresses a different point of view she will cause conflict and the avoidance of conflict is more important than how she feels.

2. Physical violence and controlling behaviour involves attacks on or threats of attack on one's physical safety and integrity. These range from hitting, kicking, punching and assault with weapons, through to murder. It can involve harming or threatening to harm children, relatives, pets or possessions. . . .

3. Verbal violence and controlling behaviour includes verbal putdowns and ridicule of any aspect of a woman's being, such as her body, her beliefs, occupation, cultural background, skills, friends or family.

4. Sexual violence and controlling behaviour includes all sexual behaviour without consent (or threats of such behaviour), such as unwanted touching, rape, exposing himself and making her view pornography. It also includes a man expecting a woman to have sex as a form of reconciliation after he has just beaten her; in these circumstances she is unable to withhold consent for fear of further violence.

5. Social violence or controlling behaviour includes all behaviour which limits, controls or interferes with a woman's social activities or relationships with others, such as controlling her movements and denying her access to her family and friends.

6. Financial violence and controlling behaviour includes not giving a woman access to her share of the shared resources, expecting her to manage the household on an impossibly low amount of money, and criticism and blame of her when she is unable to.

7. Spiritual violence or controlling behaviour includes all behaviour which denigrates a woman's religious or spiritual beliefs and preventing her from attending religious gatherings or practising her faith. It also includes harming or threatening to harm women or children in religious or occult rituals.

8. Other controlling behaviour refers to other methods used to control women that do not fit the above descriptions or may not in itself appear to be violent but that deny a woman's right to autonomy and equality, especially when used frequently or

in combination with violence. This includes telling her what to do and not allowing her to carry out her own wishes, as for example, arriving too late to look after the children when she wants to do something of which he disapproves.

Although forms of *religious violence* can fall into the above categories, religious violence deserves its own category. Forcing a woman to attend a church preferred by her husband and not allowing her to continue in her own faith is abusive. Obligating her to convert to Christianity when she already has a faith belief is disrespectful. Verbal abuse, such as calling her a demon or telling her she will go to hell because she refuses to accept her husband's faith certainly falls within this category. Perhaps the worst form of religious abuse is telling someone to tolerate suffering or abuse in the name of Christ because that is how she can share in "carrying the cross."

THE CONCEPT OF FAMILY

Family traditionally includes a biological family as well as those who live with or relate intimately to members of a given household. This may include a live-in boyfriend or girlfriend. It may include ex-spouses to whom the family needs to relate for the children's sake. The dwelling together of an extended family is very normal within several ethnic groups living in the United States and other countries as well. Occasionally, even three or four generations may live together in one household. By contrast, over the last three decades social-service and government institutions have been forced to recognize single mothers with children as heads of households. Throughout this book the definition of family includes nuclear families (those with a father, mother, and children present), single mothers with children, fathers or older siblings as heads of households, children living with grandparents or guardians, and partners (same-sex or male-female) with or without children.

Various definitions of family are used by political, religious, and cultural entities, according to their need or function. This has produced what Chilean professor of philosophy Olga Grau Duhart calls the "phenomenon of hyper-representation" of family.[27] Today the word *family* has different meanings and functions. Traditionally, family has meant an establishment with a hierarchical structure in which members follow culturally determined roles. A family is usually the first hierarchical structure that human beings encounter. The word itself originates from its Latin root, *familia*, as in the Greco-Roman *paterfamilias*, which refers to all the slaves and servants belonging to the *pater* (father) in the house. All those who belong to the family submit to the will of the father, who is the chief of the house. This understanding reflected the patriarchal household value of the government.[28] Thus, the concept of family, which mirrored the political ideology of the republic, served a supporting role.

Grau Duhart offers new insights into how *family* might be perceived when she defines the family unit as "an affectionate climate," a style of living together, and a normative space from which to look at institutions.[29] She examines how the family functions, how it changes, and how it is influenced and manipulated by outside institutions. The concept of family in the United States varies widely because of the many different ethnic constructs that are present. Traditionally, the family has been considered a fundamental unit in the organization of society. A definition with religious overtones sees *family* as "those who descend from one common progenitor; a tribe, clan, or race; kindred; house; as, the human family; the family of Abraham; the father of a family." Perhaps the most useful American definition is "a group of kindred or closely related individuals."

Some definitions of *family* have economic, sociological, or psychological implications. In the clinical and counseling arena, for example, *family* refers to one's family of origin, including parents and siblings as well as spouse and children.[30] *Family* has also been defined as "any group of people related biologically, emotionally, or legally." In 1948 the United Nations defined family as "the natural and fundamental group unit of society and its entitled protection by society and State." During the last two decades, in particular, the definition of *family* has rapidly expanded to include single parents, bi-racial couples, blended families, unrelated individuals living cooperatively, and homosexual couples, among others.[31] In 2005 the National Institute of Mental Health defined family as a "network of mutual commitment" in order to accommodate the new structures that are part of the realities of families today. In the United States today it is often lifestyles and personal choices that define a family.

While the most helpful definitions of *family* are those that aim at being descriptive and inclusive of all types of families, many definitions have an underlying motive that moves the concept of family from being descriptive to being prescriptive. This is particularly true in the religious arena, which tends to define *family* according to an ideal that is often prescriptive, which I find less helpful. When working with family violence, the aim is to point out the strength of a united family, whose quality of life is mutually nurtured and sustained, and to identify and name any violent behavior within that family as a weakness that does harm.

Religious leaders and family counselors and therapists seek to contribute in creating a culture of peace by helping families with unhealthy patterns of behavior move family members toward healthier ways of relating to one another. Christians have the essential tools based on the common law of respect and human dignity for all presented first in the Ten Commandments, which in fact form an excellent declaration of human rights.

THE ROOTS OF VIOLENCE

In learning more about the nature of violence, studies done by Colombian psychologist and seminary professor Amparo de Medina have been most helpful. She uses both a systematic and a linear approach in dealing with this problem and its multiple causes. In *Libres de la violencia familiar* (free from violence in the family), she presents research developed in 1987 by the Commission of Studies of Violence in Colombia. The commission stated that violence is a two-way process in the struggle for power in which the weak one being abused mistreats the one with power, and the person with power takes advantage of the weak.[32] This research argues that there is violence within the one who imposes domination, and there is also violence within those who challenge this control.[33] From a feminist perspective, however, we have rightly learned to be cautious because such an approach tends to increase the victimization of women. When there is an imbalance of power, the weaker is always more vulnerable, and this means women in most of the cases and children at all times.

Cases of domestic violence also involve what Jorge Corsi of Argentina, a leading expert on family violence, calls "cross violence," which occurs when a couple hits each other.[34] Because violence produces violence, the woman eventually strikes back after being abused for a period of time. In reported cases, women raised in violent homes may have the tendency to repeat this pattern.

What occasionally provokes women to respond with violence toward their abusers can be described as *internalized oppression*, a term more often used by scholars who analyze racism. In addition to the worthless feeling that oppression produces in victims, internalized oppression affects their psyche in such a way that they are prone to be violent within their families and even with others of their own gender. This includes women who use violent behavior with other women, with their own children, with their intimate partners, and with their physical surroundings. After years of being abused, oppression may produce violent behavior in abused women as a direct result of the internalized oppression they have lived with. As a Latina who has lived in the minority sector of several American cities, I have seen the aggressive behavior of Latinos against members of their own ethnic group and also against blacks, and the same behavior exhibited within the black ethnic group. This results from the oppression suffered by all minority groups in the United States. Violence is a learned behavior.

There are also women who emotionally and physically abuse their spouses or partners; however, national statistics on adult domestic violence continue to show that only 5 percent of the victims of abuse are men (although this percentage is growing) while 95 percent are women. In any case, both men and women can be victims of violence, and in many cases the children whose eyes and ears witness violent incidents at home become secondary victims. Professor Medina notes that violence is a result of a social context that not only tolerates violence but also justifies it.[35] Toleration and justification of violence are often key in reproducing violence.

A THEOLOGY OF NONVIOLENCE

Christian peace theology and a theology of nonviolence are both present within the biblical concept of *shalom*, which is understood as peaceful well-being and justice. *Shalom* can include peace with God, peace with self, peace with neighbor, and peace with the environment. In order to have a richer sense of *shalom*, its spiritual meaning must also include political, economic, and social justice. Peace theology has a continuum of practices, one of which is nonviolence. I have chosen to walk a path of nonviolence, believing that nonviolence is the truest expression of peace theology and that it is constitutive of shalom. Some believers in peace as a Christian practice may not choose to express their stances in nonviolent ways and may limit their actions to nonresistance. However, as a peacemaker, I believe that God calls Christians to engage in nonviolent action. Thus, when I use *a theology of nonviolence* throughout this book, I am referring to the specific way of bringing peaceful resolution through active nonviolence.

The kin-dom of God exists in the sharing of sisterhood and brotherhood within a community of faith. In the early church the brothers and sisters who worshiped together understood that the kin-dom of God was present in the way believers lived together in peace, in mutual exhortation, and in the sharing of both material goods and spiritual blessings.

Many churches today in North America are heavily influenced by a strong Pentecostal current or charismatic movement, including churches attached to the "gospel of prosperity." Even mainstream Protestant churches have suffered divisions because of the so-called Spirit movement.[36] This seems to indicate that people are searching for something different, something that has not been previously available, perhaps a feeling or an emotion that will fill their emptiness or alleviate their internal pains and struggles. Phoebe, a friend of mine who is a victim of domestic violence, moved from the Baptist faith in which she was raised to the Bahai faith, then to Roman Catholicism, and finally to a large charismatic church. Today she admits to feeling invisible, but she also feels useful through work in the church's social-action program. Today people who are looking for something different to fill their spiritual needs are not hesitant to move from one faith community to another. Many of these people include wounded women and their children who are searching for a safe spiritual home. What do our churches have to offer them? In addition, some Anabaptist Mennonites, members of traditional peace churches, have abandoned their peace heritage with its rich theology of nonviolence. As a result of these trends, some peace churches are not actively offering nonviolence theology as a practical tool for Christian living. In these churches, family life has suffered.

During the last five decades, social and economic conflicts have motivated our Anabaptist leaders to rethink how the theology of peace can help the church respond to the many crises in the world. While many religious leaders have used the just-war theory[37] to support action in World War I and World War II, the Korean War, the Vietnam War, the Gulf War, and the Iraq War, Mennonites throughout history have practiced active nonviolence by walking with war-torn communities and confronting injustices. Nonviolence is not new to our time. Rosa Parks, Martin Luther King, Jr., and many other leaders in the civil rights movement were firm believers and practitioners of nonviolent resistance.

Nevertheless, nonviolent responses have not always been viewed as the course for activism. In the German-Swiss Mennonite tradition of the nineteenth century, U.S. Mennonites became the "quiet in the land," practicing nonresistance and keeping themselves separate and uninvolved in current issues. However, in his article "Can We Make Sense of Mennonite Peace Theology?" John R. Burkholder reminds us that "liberation nonviolence calls for increased involvement in achieving the goals of justice, peace, salvation and reconciliation."[38] During the history of the Mennonite Church, Mennonite peace theology has ranged from nonresistance to pacifism, terms that cover a wide spectrum of Mennonite views about peace theology. There are undoubtedly similar journeys in other peace churches as well as in the traditional Protestant churches and the Catholic Church that embrace a particular peace theology in their life and ministry. However, since the 1970s, biblical beliefs on nonviolence have been seen as an integral part of peace theology in the Mennonite tradition.

Peace theology is also influenced by the social location and personal experience of theologians and of the receiving communities. It may have quite a different shape in the United States, Canada, Nicaragua, and Kenya. John R. Burkholder and Barbara Nelson Gingerich have summarized the diversity of thought and practice within peace theology, addressing issues pertinent to their times. It is not surprising that issues such as war, taxes used to support war, the draft, and foreign-policy decisions about third-world poverty have dictated the focus of particular peace theologies.[39] But none has dealt with the violence present in the private order of families. I maintain that a theology of nonviolence and peace has much to say about domestic violence, which is a family, community, and societal problem; churches can and should take an active role in ending violence within families by teaching the practices of nonviolence as biblical principles.

During the 1980s some traditional peace churches (Mennonites, Quakers, Church of the Brethren, and others) came together to address common worldwide issues. As part of the wider ecumenical movement, peace churches had been participating in the Fellowship of Reconciliation, which brought together leaders from the American Baptist Church, the Presbyterian Church, the Reformed Church, the

Disciples of Christ, the Mennonites, and the Quakers, among others. They unified efforts to respond to the wars in Central America and to foster better relations with our sisters and brothers in Cuba. The Mennonite Central Committee (an eighty-five-year-old development and relief organization of the Mennonites, Mennonite Brethren, and Brethren in Christ churches in the United States and Canada) has been a key instrument in promoting these initiatives.

In addition to seeking peace in situations of conflict and war, Anabaptists have searched for an ecclesiology that will help create the community of faith and shalom that God expects of us. Anabaptist Juan Driver has developed an ecclesiology with vital possibilities for us today in America that is in harmony with the theology of peace and nonviolence. He advocates a church that understands its mandate for here and now, and he speaks of a radical vision relevant for today's social, political, and economic reality.

Driver's vision offers a liberating reading of the Hebrew Bible and of our times, showing how the church can participate in the salvific project of God. Driver's work shows how radically Jesus lived his life and how the messianic community of the first century understood God's call through Jesus and lived those principles of peace. Driver sees the need for the churches to embrace a radical new ecclesiology that reflects the implications of being a church of Jesus Christ in the world.[40] His message is clear and practical, using illustrations from his vast experience working with many churches in the United States, Latin America, and Spain. He is concise in advocating that a missional community must be intentional in proclaiming that the kin-dom of God has arrived and that Christ's reign must be present in the way we live that call. God desires a kin-dom in which interpersonal relationships correspond to the divine intentions of God expressed in the covenant with Moses (Lv 26:3–6). With courage, the messianic community must confront the world's injustices present in the wider community. However, and more important, we must seek justice for the people closest to us, that is, our family. We must be alert to the false values that foster pretense and domination. On the contrary, the community of Christ must incarnate the true values of the kin-dom of God.[41] Driver reminds us that "the church is not the kin-dom. It is, rather, the messianic community in the service of the kin-dom. . . .In the church's life and values, it anticipates the kin-dom."[42]

Churches need to remember that their mandate is to opt for life, recognizing that this has enormous consequences for all of humanity.

Christians are called not only to resist evil but also to create and live out a viable alternative, and this includes life within the family. All Christian families should examine in what ways they reflect gospel values and how they might relate to one another in kindness and love inside the privacy of their homes. And it is important to remember that evil and violence can come about through human actions but also through neglect. Time must be set aside and devoted to cultivating relationships within families.

Our Anabaptist foremothers and forefathers of the Radical Reformation in the sixteenth century advocated a concrete and personal experience of salvation. This was a salvation with an important communal expression that was obedient to the teachings of Jesus and imitated the first-century Christian community. This Anabaptist model of restoration was very supportive of family and of close communal relationships.

IMPROVING THE QUALITY OF LIFE IN THE FAMILY

How can the quality of life in families that suffer from violence be improved when the privacy of the family is revered today in our country? Will family members allow outsiders to come in and witness or question violent behavior? To begin with, disagreement on various social and cultural levels about what constitutes violent behavior makes it difficult to confront or change such behaviors. Although there are laws that spell out what is harmful behavior, groups and individuals often will not admit the presence of violence in their homes because they feel "everything is normal here." A sound quality of life in a family should include the absence of abuse, violent behavior, and forms of injury among all members of that family; this goes beyond the mere nonexistence of conflict.

A member of my church once told me that her husband, who had total control of the family's money, would punish her by not giving money to her or her children to take the bus to go to church on Sunday. This certainly qualifies as abusive behavior. Should the church—or I as a member of the church—speak out or take a position? If the home is a continuation or part of the church community, then should we enter the "sacred space" within the family? In order to break the cycle of violence, we must speak out and protect those who are suffering or are in danger, confronting the problem with an attitude of love.

Sociologists Richard Gelles and Murray Straus, widely known for their research into domestic violence, describe the inequality of women and children in relation to men as one of the leading causes of violence in family life. One of the many faces of this inequality is poverty, which is highly visible across many cultures today. In Colombia, 69 percent of the population lives in poverty. Of this group, 20 percent live in absolute misery; over half of these are women.[43] In rural Zimbabwe and throughout most of Africa women are responsible for most of the production and processing of food crops, while men control the means of production. In Japan and other countries in Asia women are taught to obey their fathers when they are unmarried, their husbands when married, and to be under the protection of their sons when old. In the United States and other developed countries, for women of color (Latinas, Asians, women of African descent, and Native Americans) this inequality is often triply expressed in sexist, racist, and classist attitudes.

SIGNS OF VIOLENCE PRESENT IN US

As we examine closely the leaves of this tree of family violence, we can see the texture of the leaves, the veins that provide nourishment, and also the structure that lies beneath the surface. Within human beings, there is also an underlying structure that has many elements, including the tendency to reproduce violence. When we are exposed to it, we somehow seem to become contaminated with its germs.

In *The Abuse of Power: A Theological Problem*, James Newton Poling, a theologian specializing in pastoral care, describes his experience in assisting women and children who have been victims of abuse and his experience in assisting the offenders. Poling describes the resilience and the hope he has seen in those who were once victims and who today are celebrating their survival.[44] Even in the midst of violence they have experienced or may be experiencing in their families, it has still been possible for them to "bounce back up." The National Network for Family Resiliency notes that family resiliency is "the family's ability to cultivate strengths to positively meet the challenges of life."[45] When working on the complex issue of family violence, it is important to recognize that the family is a structure in which domination and control create conditions for abuse. We human beings have the power both to nurture and at the same time to hurt others by words and by actions.

As a mother of two young girls, I must confess that on occasion my humanity has influenced me to lift my hand and, in a spirit of correction, hit them. The force of my adult hand on the vulnerable and weak arm of my younger child produced a dislocation of her delicate bones in the spring of 1998. I inflicted this on her while expressing my anger after she had slapped my face. I am responsible for my violent action. In my Puerto Rican culture, it is considered a great offense if a person slaps your face, and a sign of particular disrespect if a child does this to a parent. I recognize that I reacted out of anger and that my embedded culture of violence rose instantaneously within me. I did not try to justify my actions to the nurse in the doctor's office. I explained all that had happened and that I was deeply ashamed of my actions. I am still amazed at how I, a person who believes in peacemaking, could do this to my child.

In order for evil to be overcome, we must face the tendency in ourselves and in others to use power in evil ways. Only when we face the depth of our own ambiguity—that both good and evil are present within us—will we discover the resilient hope that power can be used with justice. As well stated by Poling, "Only when we confess the abuse of power in our lives, confront the abuse of power in others, repent of its evil, and commit ourselves anew to justice and righteousness will the possibility of evil be contained."[46]

The spiral of violence also moves the definition of *violence* to a deeper level. Forces within society today seem to perpetuate violence, turning it into a spiral that sinks lower and lower.[47] When we sense an injury to our person, we often turn to inflict injury on another. Our hope is that we are conscious of this pull and the need for awareness every day to resist the spiral with nonviolent strategies and in the end overcome it.

A first step is to search for a new definition of *love*, one that moves away from a love that tolerates abuse. Any concept of God we have learned that involves a God who calls us to suffer is distorted and needs to be dismantled. This certainly includes an omnipotent God who encourages victims to suffer in silence from the evil of others. Jesus brought life, not death, to those who suffer. We need to discover a "God of love and power who is not patriarchal and does not encourage victims to suffer."[48] A father who beats the mother or a mother who hits her children does not image a loving God. Such individuals must begin an intensive healing process so they image instead a God who is compassionate, loving, and forgiving.

THE ROLE OF THE CHURCH

Do churches have the courage to begin examining this evil of domestic violence? To do so will involve a willingness to examine critically a church's own complicity in violence against women, children, and others who are vulnerable in society. Once a community of faith understands its own complicity, it must dismantle it and then become a resource of healing for those who are hurt and damaged by the abuse of power. I believe firmly that all churches are called to encourage their members to live the values of the kin-dom of God each day, stating clearly that violence in our lives is unacceptable. Churches around the world must be willing to support and at times intervene when family violence is suspected or evident.[49] As Poling states, "Abuse of power is a theological problem."[50]

How can churches advocate for peace in families that suffer violence in the privacy of their homes? In the Hebrew Bible, the concept of *shalom*, or peace, is holistic; it describes the state of well-being that God wants for all people. Such well-being refers not only to physical conditions but also to harmony in relationships within the community. It begins with taking care of those who are not provided for, including orphans, widows, and foreigners (Dt 10:18). Given the injustices that the people of Israel were perpetuating toward their own kind, God's desire for harmony in relationships was a message of confrontation from prophets like Jeremiah, Ezekiel, and Amos.

Ezekiel expressed an important message to the royal courts when he described them with the words, "They have misled my people, saying 'Peace,' when there is no peace" (13:10). The prophet Jeremiah also warned the people: "They have treated the wound of my people carelessly, saying, 'Peace, peace,' when there is no peace" (6:14). However, the problem went beyond that of simply declaring peace when there was no war; the internal condition of the nation itself was not one of *shalom*. The peace proclaimed by the prophets was a state of *shalom* that was based on internal and external harmony with one's self, with God-Sophia,[51] and with the rest of humanity. At the time of the prophets, authentic peace, the living in harmony required by Yahweh, was usually absent.

An analogy can be made between the Israelite community at the time of the prophets and the conditions in which Christian families live today in the privacy of their homes. The desire for peace is often overwhelmed by internal chaos, which can take the form of illness, poverty, lack of time, or unemployment. As faith communities we must develop a clear ministry toward families in order to walk with them, to help them identify the roots of the conflict and violence they experience, and to support them in their journey as Christians who deserve to live the *shalom* that God-Sophia intends for all people, with a quality of life in which daily problems and conflicts are solved peacefully. God's plan for salvation and *shalom* are good news that must be brought to these families.

The peace to which the prophets referred was the peace promised to them in the covenant between God and God's people given to Moses: "If you follow my statutes and keep my commandments and observe them . . . I will grant peace in the land, and you shall lie down, and no one shall make you afraid; . . . and no sword shall go through your land" (Lv 26:3–6). The purpose of the Law given to Moses was to teach the people that all were to be treated justly; a life lived in *shalom* meant equality for all.

God-Sophia also hears the cry of wives oppressed under the domination of violent husbands, just as God-Sophia is sensitive to the cry of a vulnerable child who may be physically injured or sexually molested by a family member. In this same way the church should be prepared to hear the cries and become involved in the lives of families who are suffering. If younger members of the community of faith do not live in peace in the supposedly safe environment of their homes, then we, the church, become accomplices to the sins committed against them. The prophets' message to Christian churches today is that it is time for us to live our theology of nonviolence actively, starting at home. While our first task as churches is to create awareness of the violence that affects our families, we must not stop there. We must embark on the enterprise of constructing a model of being Christian families who know how to live in harmony, incarnating holistic peace.

SIGNS OF DESPAIR AND SIGNS OF HOPE

Because manifestations of the epidemic of violence are so devastating today, we must examine whether the theology of nonviolence of Jesus presents a viable and practical solution for this social ailment. The story of Mary, a survivor of violence, can demonstrate how her peace church journeyed with her toward healing. While interviewers usually change the names of subjects in order to protect their privacy, Mary told me she wanted to keep her name because her healing journey moved her from feeling bitter to feeling the glory of God shine in her life again.

Mary's life has not been easy; in fact, it has been a hard road to travel, particularly when at age forty she discovered she had been sexually abused as a child not once but several times by male relatives. (It is not uncommon for victims of sexual abuse to remove such traumatic experiences from their memory.) By age forty she had a seventeen-year-old son and a twenty-year-old daughter. She described her marriage as "not good" because she hated the sexual intimacy and was using all the excuses in the book to say no to sex. She knew her sexuality was not dead but severely "wounded." After a frightening experience in which she felt herself attracted to another man, she convinced her husband that both of them should attend a Marriage Encounter weekend, a Christian retreat for couples to evaluate their relationship and work at strengthening their marriage vows. She cried from the moment she arrived at the retreat. Her primary discovery was that she had never learned to love herself. Grateful for the prayers of the retreat leaders, she finished the retreat in a more hopeful spirit.

The evening Mary returned from the retreat, as she was unpacking books that had arrived at her office, she came across one entitled *Child Abuse and Hope for Healing*. She began reading and, as she read descriptions of the signs of abuse, she recognized herself. She could identify many of those signs present in her life: depression; continual body aches, including backaches and headaches; and the presence of a constant knot in her stomach. This was in the spring of 1989. She began to give voice to what had happened in her childhood, identifying the abusers. Mary experienced a great relief, realizing that her forty-year-old secret could no longer remain silent. She proceeded to seek out safe places where she could share her story with supportive friends and receive pastoral care and counseling.

Then Mary asked a Christian counselor from the church if he knew of any Christian support groups for abused women in the area. Learning that none was available, Mary, with the advice of the counselor, started a support group. Mary's pastor opened the church for the group, and the women began to meet weekly. Mary was grateful for her pastor's understanding and support, and even his willingness, at Mary's suggestion, to preach about domestic violence. While women are not allowed to preach in her church, the pastor gave her time during the sermon to describe her work helping women recover from sexual abuse they suffered as children. The pastor later delegated several couples to counsel a young married couple that was going through the wife's struggle with the pain associated with sexual abuse during her childhood.

Mary was fortunate to have a supportive husband who entered into the healing process and who encouraged her to use her experience to help other women. He advised her not to "waste her pain." In the years that followed, she, together with women professionals, was instrumental in assisting her larger church body to form a committee to address issues of abuse, recovery, and prevention, including accountability for church leaders who themselves were sexual offenders.

Today, in her mid-fifties, Mary has collaborated in developing materials on the theme of sexual abuse and family violence for her wider faith community; she leads groups for men who batter their partners/wives; and she continues to share her story. And, in a humble way, she recognizes that while she is not totally healed, she is healed enough to be an instrument of healing for others.

2

Branches That Connect

Some Dimensions of the Problem

The next step we must take is to look carefully at the presence of violence in order to understand exactly what is happening. In the previous chapter we looked at the leaves, the visible presence of violence within families. It is now time to look at the branches that support and sustain the leaves. These branches include a number of cultural, social, economic, psychological, and historical factors that influence violent behavior within families. This form of analysis, which is used to understand the reality of any situation, can be called *contextual* or *social*. The following story provides many clues about one social context for people affected by family violence.

A COMMON STORY

When we were living in Armenia, Colombia, two women friends, Jessica and Carmen,[1] joined me for lunch in our home. Carmen was weeping, crying out of a deep pain that had been in her heart for the last fifteen years of her marriage. She could not control her tears and felt ashamed of her sobbing. As she wiped away her tears, she told her story. "I cannot forget the day he came in drunk, accusing me of liking another man. He put a gun to my head, right here [pointing to the back part of her head], and said that he wanted to kill me. I screamed at him, telling him to go ahead and kill me because I didn't want to live anymore. On occasions I have even tried to kill myself, but my two boys have convinced me not to."

Soon after that Carmen began baptismal classes in the church we had joined. While her husband, David, was raised in a Christian home, he struggled with alcoholism. It was hard for him to manage his disease and live a Christian life.

Carmen's story was not new to me. It is a story that makes the headlines far too often throughout Latin America, where many forms of violence toward women seem to have become a normal part of the culture. It is also a familiar story in the United States. When I read of these cases where I live, I am always tempted to confront the abusive husband and go into the home to try to fix the problem, or to empower the wife, as I was trained to do when I worked in YWCA sexual-assault centers in Indiana and Pennsylvania. What should church people do in such situations?

On the other side of the table sat Jessica, who had an abusive father. She listened in silence to Carmen's cry for help; she understood because she privately shared a similar pain. Although in the last decade Jessica's family had made a commitment to join the church, her family members came from a background where violent treatment was considered to accompany love. When Jessica was finishing high school, her father would follow her to school. He was unemployed in those years and jealous of any relationships Jessica had with young men. When she returned home after school, he would question her harshly and then hit her. She would cry out: "Why do you hurt me? Is it that you want me sexually?" She lived in constant fear of her father, and their relationship was filled with tension.

Such extreme jealousy and possessiveness exist and are considered normal in some patriarchal societies in which women and children are deemed to be the property of a man. In some such cultures fathers or other males in the household are allowed to manifest their anger, and even their insecurities, through physical and emotional violence toward wives and daughters.

Would confronting Carmen's husband or Jessica's father stop the violence? Can these relationships be restored? What are the needs of individuals and families who experience such explosions of gender-based, overt and covert violence in the home? As Christians, how can we call attention to these behaviors and walk with people in order to help the families?

SOCIAL ANALYSIS

One of the most important principles to understand about violence is that those who live in a violent culture generally produce violent behavior. A group of psychologists, neurophysiologists, and anthropologists gathered in Seville, Spain, in 1986 to study issues of violence and war. Their final report, called the Seville Statement, asserts that human beings are not genetically programmed for war or other forms of violent behavior, although they do have the capability to act violently. They described the nature of violence and war in the following way:

Believing that it is our responsibility to address from our particular disciplines the most dangerous and destructive activities of our species, violence and war . . . we, the undersigned scholars from around the world and from relevant sciences, have met and arrived at the following Statement on Violence. In it, we challenge a number of alleged biological findings that have been used, even by some in our disciplines, to justify violence and war. . . .

It is scientifically incorrect to say that we have inherited a tendency to make war from our animal ancestors. . . . Warfare is a peculiarly human phenomenon and does not occur in other animals.

The fact that warfare has changed so radically over time indicates that it is a product of culture. . . . There are cultures which have not engaged in war for centuries, and there are cultures which have engaged in war frequently at some times and not at others. . . .

It is scientifically incorrect to say that humans have a "violent brain." While we do have the neural apparatus to act violently . . . [h]ow we act is shaped by how we have been conditioned and socialized. . . .

It is scientifically incorrect to say that war is caused by "instinct" or any single motivation. . . . Modern war involves institutional use of personal characteristics such as obedience, suggestibility, and idealism, social skills such as language, and rational considerations such as cost-calculation, planning, and information processing. The technology of modern war has exaggerated traits associated with violence both in the training of actual combatants and in the preparation of support for war in the general population. As a result of this exaggeration, such traits are often mistaken to be the causes rather than the consequences of the process. . . .

We conclude that biology does not condemn humanity to war, and that humanity can be . . . empowered with confidence to undertake the transformative tasks needed in this International Year of Peace and in the years to come. Although these tasks are mainly institutional and collective, they also rest upon the consciousness of individual participants for whom pessimism and optimism are crucial factors. Just as "wars begin in the minds of men," peace also begins in our minds. The same species who invented war is capable of inventing peace. The responsibility lies with each of us.

(Signed in Seville, 16 May 1986 by twenty scientists and subsequently adopted by UNESCO at the twenty-fifth session of the General Conference on 16 November 1989.)[2]

This declaration states clearly that violent action by humans constitutes learned behavior for ways of dealing with their sense of insecurity, feeling threatened by the situation surrounding them, and wanting to be in control. While violent behavior is often categorized as an anger issue, its roots lie in the intentionality of the behavior. Violence is a choice, just as peace is a choice.

THE CULTURAL FACTOR OF PATRIARCHY

What is not described in the Seville Statement is the presence in most violent societies today of patriarchy. Patriarchy, called at times a monster or a web to indicate both its power and its scope, produces individuals, both men and women, who perpetuate the system by socializing children with concepts of masculinity and femininity that give power and control to men and manipulate and oppress women and children. In many ways patriarchy parallels the ideology of Manifest Destiny that led the United States to intervene in the affairs of other countries, such as the Sandinista-Contra war in Nicaragua and civil wars in El Salvador, Guatemala, Argentina, and Chile, and the war today in Iraq. Patriarchy nurtures social and psychological phenomena that seem to be expressed by controlling and intervening whenever possible.

In "Cultural Violence against Women in Latin America," feminist theologian and scripture scholar Elsa Tamez makes a strong argument for feminists' need to analyze and understand cultural values as a prerequisite to overcoming violence against women. Tamez emphasizes the identification of values within a culture that proceed from tradition, as well as those values that are common denominators in all cultures. But, as Tamez remarks, it is essential that women "defend those cultural values which help them resist with dignity the attacks of a hegemonic cultural imposition which only seeks its own economic and political interests and which is sustained by the 'kyriarchal' pyramid."[3]

Analysis with a feminist lens helps to clarify the underlying issue of the masculine use of power to control, which derives primarily from the heavy influence of patriarchy on both women and men. This is particularly true of Latino cultures. In *El lado oculto de la masculinidad: Tratamiento para ofensores* (the shadow side of masculinity, treatment for offenders), Gioconda Batres Méndez, a well-known psychiatrist from Costa Rica with professional experience in modifying the violent behavior of abusive men, writes, "Patriarchy turns us [women] into thankful victims making sure that both man and woman reproduce the same system."[4] In other words, women often find comfort in passivity, in feeling provided for and protected. Patriarchy also provides benefits for men, who feel useful through providing and being responsible for others. (Some would maintain that, after all, this is what the Bible says!) She points out that a patriarchal society has the power to socialize men to be controlling husbands and fathers through its cultural practices. The idea of masculinity taught requires a man to be strong, forceful, and better than a woman. These values appear to be present in all patriarchal societies.[5]

It is important to recognize that family violence is not just an emotional or psychological problem; at its worst it also puts the lives of others—mostly women and children—at risk. Jorge Corsi, a professor at the University of Buenos Aires, notes that investigations of violence in the family have encountered two basic variables related to the distribution of power—gender and age—both of which place women and children at high risk.[6] In his words: "Power has been conferred on men, which the culture assigns to them by the fact of being male, designating them as head of the home or family. . . . Soon this power is reflected in interpersonal relations . . . through an abusive use of that power. . . . The husband perceives the woman or the children as his property, and that means he has the right to do with them whatever he wants."[7]

Throughout Latin America, such male domination is known as machismo. Although this concept comes from the Spanish word *macho* and is primarily spoken of in Latino cultures, Anglo-Saxons have their own version of this prototypical male. Corsi writes that "this traditional masculine model is composed of external characteristics such as to make, to demonstrate, to achieve, etc. This model does not give much importance to the inner life of feelings or the expression of emotions. Their identity is based on repressing emotions."[8]

María Cristina Palacios has written extensively about patriarchal culture. She sees the breakdown of the family system as a result of the corruption of the political and social systems in which families live.[9] But she goes behind that facade to emphasize the role patriarchal culture plays in defining what a *family* is. In her words, "It is within family structures that the social order is reproduced and the domination/subordination attitude is validated; once these codes are broken, the insertion of violence becomes part of the family dynamics."[10] Palacios makes a strong call for not holding the family responsible for the violence in today's society. She concludes that family violence does not result from a decline of values or the disintegration of the traditional family unit; nor does she blame women who have joined the work force.[11] Indeed, some fundamentalists and several current pro-family movements maintain that a major cause of the crisis American families are facing today is women joining the work force rather than staying at home. Such movements call for men to reassert their authority and to reclaim their lost space in the household. Such an approach does not help but rather can turn a home into a struggle for power.

Instead, Palacios lists three main factors that affect the family: (1) social relationships characterized by the use of a hierarchical power and the use of discrimination to support domination and oppression; (2) destabilization of the social order produced by so many crimes and the easy availability of firearms; and (3) capitalistic and consumer pressures to become modernized and have consumer goods, which bring rapid change to society.[12]

Social contexts that accept violence as natural demonstrate how their members are shaped by the powerful octopus of patriarchy, whose tentacles reach out to destroy the divine nature of equality between genders. North American feminist theologian Marie Fortune is an expert on family violence and has written extensively on the abuse of women and children. Her theological insightfulness on themes such as justice and restorative process in congregations is a true gift for those of us that respond to the call of victims and their families. Fortune offers three goals that can guide ministers in making a better pastoral response to violence. "(1) Protection of the victim from further abuse; (2) stopping the abuser's violence; and (3) restoration of family or mourning the loss of the relationship."[13] Fortune advises that the successful accomplishment of the first two goals will determine which outcome of the third goal, restoration or loss, will occur. "To ignore goals #1 and #2 would preclude any possibility of a genuine healing of the relationship."[14]

SOCIAL AND ECONOMIC FACTORS

Álvaro A. Fernández Gallego, a professor of anthropology at the University of Quindío in Colombia, is another specialist on violence. He notes the diversity of theories of violence that exist, especially those guided primarily by the goal of filling an empirical void. Theorists in this category are preoccupied with answering the why of violence but neglect addressing how violence shapes and forms social relationships.[15] However, his vast study of the phenomenon of violence raises questions about traditional paradigms, such as the belief that family violence is a direct product of violence in society or that violence in the family causes violence in the streets. The core question in his studies is the presence of violence in interpersonal relationships, in the family, and among siblings, rather than where or how it originates. With his particular focus, he suggests the causes of violence lie in how we relate to each other.

In the United States violence is present in many forms. Our nation is currently fighting a war in the Middle East, and support for that war is steadily eroding, leading to disagreements among groups of people, including our elected representatives, and even within families. There is also war on the streets in our cities, with substantial increases in violent crimes in cities such as Oakland, Phoenix, and Orlando. While there is data on the legal sale of firearms to private owners, there is no data available on the numbers of weapons on the

street because of the illegal market in unregistered guns. A vivid example of senseless killing happened on October 2, 2006, in Lancaster
County, Pennsylvania, when a seemingly normal white working-class
man who possessed a number of weapons entered an Amish school
and shot four children and a teaching assistant before killing himself.
Other school shootings have horrified the nation, which at times appears remarkably blasé about inner-city crime; while students are
screened for weapons, the large number of weapons on the streets is
not being addressed. Going back to Gallego's perspective, could it be
that people's personal value systems have deteriorated internally? We
need to recognize that individual lives are influenced by both internal
and external factors. As Gallego reminds us, violence is a multifaceted
phenomenon.

Social worker Angela Maria Quintero has studied the different factors that promote family violence in society, especially in the areas of
abuse of children and neglect of the elderly. She names the first influ-
ential factor "the culture of war and blood" and claims this is transmitted ideologically.[16] Although one can argue that Quintero speaks
from her experience living in Colombia, South America, in an almost
fifty-year war, the same can be said of what we experience here in the
United States. Her claim that ideology plays a subtle but powerful
force in promoting violence is validated by the all-too-common U.S.
belief that we have the right to attack others and American feelings of
superiority over other cultural groups. These factors resemble the
bottom of an iceberg; while we cannot see them, they are nonetheless
present.

WHO's 2002 report on violence and health describes violence as
both "predictable and preventable" in certain environments and cau-
tions social-services agencies to see warnings in the presence of these
factors.[17] This is true of developed countries like the United States
and also of less developed countries around the world. Despite the
level of development, certain factors appear to be strong predictors of
violence within any given population. Included are individual and family factors but also rapid economic and social changes that result in a
lack of health care and educational opportunities, high unemployment
rates, and an increase in the presence of weapons. Fernández Gallego
has also identified unemployment and difficult access to institutional
resources as risk factors in family violence.[18]

The National Council on Child Abuse and Family Violence ech-
oes the WHO findings, noting that risk factors present in situations

of domestic violence often include parental substance abuse, the presence of weapons in the home, and mental health issues of family members, while the protective factors can include a protective mother, an older sibling or significant adult in the child's life, and a child's own ability to cope with stress.[19]

Violent patterns of relating to others result from the pattern within a family and also from the social model that is present in a society. If a person's experience indicates that violence is not only a viable way of solving problems but also acceptable, it is not surprising that violence will result. The vast majority of resources on family violence cite the same two reasons that family violence is so prevalent in different cultures: first, violence is permitted (and at times even encouraged); and second, violence is seldom punished. Although strong laws to prevent violence exist in the United States, some abusers still believe that they do not have to suffer the full consequences of their abusive behavior. Even the rule of law cannot always prevent a culture of violence.

It should also be noted that another significant factor that introduces stress is the increasing income gap between the poor and the wealthy, a gap that has widened dramatically over the last two decades. In addition, the currents of globalization have swept away a large number of industrial jobs that in the past had led to the growth of a strong middle class. Such external factors, many over which we have little or no control, constantly influence our lives and those of our families. It becomes our responsibility as Christians to make sure that the violence that surrounds us does not affect our relations with one another.

Social scientists describe us as products of our environment. However, as Christians, we must also remember that with faith, power, and determination, we can choose how to respond. Our tasks in this present time are to understand the causes and nature of violence, to teach younger generations to solve conflict and tension nonviolently, and to encourage older generations to unlearn patterns of patriarchy and control.

Two of the risk factors that form large branches of the tree of family violence and often interact with each other to create an environment of violence need to be described in some detail because of the significant role they play in all countries around the world: (1) poverty; and (2) other social and economic factors such as homelessness, inadequate health care, sexual abuse, and violence between intimate partners.

Poverty

While all social classes experience some level of violence, research consistently indicates that the greatest risk exists for members of the lowest socioeconomic status because they are likely to have more stressors and less access to supportive resources. The 2005 summary report of the WHO suggests that women living in poverty suffer disproportionately. According to Amnesty International, "Lack of economic autonomy, denial of property rights or access to housing, and fear of losing their children mean that few women can risk the truly daunting consequences of leaving violent situations and attempting to secure justice from a legal system that may be discriminatory or indifferent."[20] And the National Organization of Women (NOW) reports that "domestic violence rates are five times higher among families below the poverty level, and severe spouse abuse is twice as likely to be committed by unemployed men as by those working full time.[21]

It should be emphasized at the outset that poverty generally exacerbates the vulnerability of women and girls, making them easy targets for violence. Poverty often forces women to the work place where, because of their need for jobs, they become vulnerable to exploitation. The result may be severely limited options, including low and/or unfair wages, poor and/or unsafe working environments, lack of control over hours and schedules, and sexual exploitation. One study found that the socioeconomic status of neighborhoods in the United States had a greater impact on the level or risk of violence than individual household income levels.[22] Lack of employment opportunities also pushes women into prostitution and other demeaning work. WHO continues to report that in poor areas around the world hundreds of thousands of women and children are sold to sexual traffickers or as slaves for manual labor. WHO presents alarming statistics on trafficking, including, for example, 200,000 Bangladeshi women trafficked between 1990 and 1997; it reports that 45,000 to 50,000 women and children are trafficked each year into the United States.[23] During my work providing health care in poor villages in the coffee zone of Colombia, I saw many cases of such trafficking. And in Armenia, Colombia, a mother told us about strangers who would visit the villages and promise young girls jobs in other countries, offering their mothers an attractive amount of money for parental permission to take them away to a new life.

When isolation is coupled with poverty, particularly in rural areas but also in urban or suburban areas, sexual violence tends to increase. The National Sexual Violence Resource Center's *Unspoken Crimes: Sexual Assault in Rural America* reveals that sexual assault rates are four times higher in counties with large rural populations than in urban counties.[24] And it should be noted that in rural areas the prevalence of sexual assault is undoubtedly much higher than the number of cases actually reported because of informal social codes that dictate privacy in such close-knit communities. The report also notes that in isolated areas relatively accepting attitudes toward sexual violence lead victims to see the reality as normal. This is also true to some degree for Latina immigrant women, and other immigrant women as well, who may have experienced abuse as a normal part of married life in a machismo culture. For immigrant women, language can also be a barrier in seeking help. In both situations of violence—isolation by geography or by language—female victims often view the violence as a normal part of life. In all such cases "victims must be afforded a culturally relevant approach, which calls for the investment of considerable time to understand the culture and build trust."[25]

The first Latina I assisted during my volunteer hours for the domestic-violence hotline of the YWCA in Indiana is a clear example of how women immigrants in this country suffer abuse from legal citizens. The man who had saved Daisy's life when she was attempting to cross the Rio Grande between the Mexican and U.S. border stabbed Daisy in her left shoulder less than a year later. Her abuser was a Mexican man who had legal status in this country and offered to help her get started here. Daisy spoke no English and had no friends to reach out to for assistance. After her release from the hospital, another Mexican family opened its home to her to protect her from the perpetrator. Afraid of deportation, she never pressed charges against him. This happened in the late 1980s before the Violence against Women's Act that today provides some protection to some immigrant women but, unfortunately, not to all.

Other Social and Economic Factors

Other factors that lead to family violence include lack of or inadequate housing, lack of educational opportunities, and unemployment and underemployment. The Joint Center for Housing Studies of

Harvard University recently reported that nearly half of the country's lowest-income families suffer from "severe housing cost burdens" that place them at risk for homelessness. In order to keep a roof over their heads they must cut back on food, clothing, and medical care. The Harvard study notes: "Since 2005 the number of such households jumped by 1.2 million to a total of 17 million. . . . Today, one in seven U.S. households is severely housing cost-burdened." The study also found that

> five years of stagnating or declining incomes have added to hous-ing affordability problems. . . .
>
> In part, these income trends reflect the fact that the economy is producing fewer middle-wage and more low-wage jobs. As a result, a growing number of America's working families—includ-ing those employed full time or with more than one earner—has severe housing cost burdens. For example, 16 percent of low-income households are headed by a full-time worker, but a dispiriting 39 percent of these households are severely cost bur-dened. . . .
>
> Especially hard hit are families with children. . . .
>
> To cope with the high costs of housing, some households re-sort to living in small quarters or sharing space with others. . . . Los Angeles ranks as both the least affordable and the most crowded, with overcrowding affecting 12 percent of households.[26]

Fitting a family with five children into a tiny living space is sad. But this is a reality in many inner-city low-income homes. It is a common scenario for those living south of the U.S. border, but it is becoming more usual on the north side of the border as well. Even in low-in-come public housing, one parent may be employed in a local poultry factory working a thirty-six-hour week with very few benefits and the stress of not being able to meet the family's needs. Tension escalates. Unemployment and underemployment are great sources of stress as well. Many economic studies have indicated that at the U.S. mini-mum wage, a family of four cannot afford a decent house. A family's purchasing power is limited to the bare minimum. Many such work-ers have not completed high school and cannot even begin to dream about going for technical training because they are barely surviving. This produces tension among the adults living together, who try to make ends meet while feeling they can never get ahead. As children grow, their needs become greater; they also want more things—what their friends have. Along with the tension, bills accumulate, energy levels are low, and disagreements among family members increase. The burden of illness and lack of medical care hover, along with the continuous possibility of being laid off. An increasing number of people in this country are working but are still poor, according to Penn State's website on poverty in America. How can the richest country in the world be unable to meet their basic needs? More than 12 percent of its total population and almost 20 percent of all children under the age of eighteen lack medical coverage. Dr. Amy K. Glasmeier states: "Recent census estimates reveal that the population percentage considered severely poor has reached a 32–year high. Between 2000 and 2005, the percent living at half of poverty-level income increased by 26% [in the United States]." Glasmeier adds that "the descent into destitution spares no community or group in society. America's urban, suburban and rural communities are all witnesses to the growth of what adds up to the 'abject poor.'"[27]

It is important to point out that poverty is not the cause of violence in the family, nor can we say that poor people express their frustration through violence. However, poverty is a major risk factor for stress. For example, our neighbor Mike, who worked in construction, was laid off, and a few weeks later we could hear through the thin walls of our connected inner-city row house yelling and fighting between Mike and his live-in girlfriend Asia. Trying to be a good neighbor, my husband told Mike that he had overhead loud arguments and expressed his concern for Asia and their year-old baby's safety. Ashamed that we had overheard his violent language, he no longer offered his friendly smile when we greeted him from our backyard. Shortly after, he began working at a local supermarket and is again gainfully employed. We are not so naive as to believe the problems of Mike and Asia are over, but the arguing has certainly diminished and Mike is smiling and talking to us once again. The stress of poverty and/or unemployment *does* make a difference.

EMOTIONAL FACTORS:
THE ROLE OF ANGER AND LACK OF SELF-CONTROL

Recently I heard a man at my church confess that he has a problem with anger. His daughter and wife sat beside him, nodding their heads in silence as he admitted that his anger causes problems with relationships. In the end, all family members are hurt emotionally or psychologically. Anger is a normal human feeling, as the apostle Paul admits in Ephesians 4:26: "Be angry but do not sin." However, Paul advises us to have self-control, one of the fruits of the spirit (Gal 5:22).

While people working on issues of justice and peace state that occasionally they are entitled to feel and express "righteous anger," this is not what we are talking about here. They have reason to be upset about the lack of justice in the world. The concern here is with the personal frustration, misunderstandings, and lack of communication that can explode in anger. They can be self-destructive and also aimed at hurting others. This is the nature of the "anger problem" described by my fellow churchgoer and affirmed by his family. Although therapists warn that negative feelings should be expressed, they must be expressed in proper ways that do not damage others. Anger is often a reaction to a psychological hurt or threat of hurt that diminishes one's sense of self. Anger is a common human feeling, but when it is used against another or for self-destruction, it becomes dangerous.

Anger is an emotion triggered by many events in one's life, including frustration. Basic aggressive impulses are known to be part of the internal resources for survival that reside in human beings and other living creatures. However, openly negative aggression is a learned behavior that is no longer a protective mechanism but has the goal of injuring another. It can result from the emotions of fear or anger or feelings of loss of control, and it often is expressed through violent behavior.

Anger and aggression are two concepts that are related but different. While aggression can be an expression of anger, anger can also be expressed nonviolently. The goal of parents, and other adults as well, should be to socialize children and youth to learn to express their anger in nonviolent ways.

PSYCHOLOGICAL AND EMOTIONAL FACTORS

Clinical research shows that individual violence is influenced by an individual's needs and tensions as well as the needs and tensions within the family and society. For the individual, these include low self-esteem, lack of self-control, and lack of skills to achieve goals by nonviolent means, often resulting in alcohol and substance abuse and deep-seated anger.[28] The last few years we have witnessed the escalation of war in Iraq, which has introduced new stresses on military families. Families have suffered great stress from assignments to serve overseas and by repeated and extended duty rotations. Family stress has been further exacerbated by the large number of returning soldiers with severe head wounds and amputations and those suffering from post-traumatic stress disorders (PTSD). These effects will inevitably become more pronounced as the conflict continues. The Department of Veterans Affairs estimates that 12 percent to 20 percent of those who have served in Iraq suffer from PTSD. A 2004 Army study found that 16.6 percent of those returning from combat tested positive for the disorder.[29] Family-violence networks have been expressing growing concerns that returning soldiers are not getting the mental-health help they need to incorporate themselves successfully back into civilian life.

During the last thirty years, social-services agencies and women's movements responding to contexts of family violence have gained much experience and knowledge. One of the recent successes has been with intervention programs designed for men who are abusive that aim to reeducate them to change their violent behavior. Counselors have concluded that the most effective way to approach these offenders is not through techniques of anger management but rather by modifying offenders' internalized concepts of masculinity based on the use of power and control over women and children. Although religious beliefs have taught people for centuries to suppress anger, it is now accepted that anger is one of the basic human feelings but that individuals need to learn to express it in healthy ways.

In Maine, domestic-violence networks and service agencies do not employ anger-management treatment for abusers because such an approach has been proven to be not only counterproductive but also dangerous. Because it does not result in rehabilitation, it offers false hope to the victim and manipulates the victim to continue the relationship. Attorney Molly Butler Bailey argues that sentencing abusers to anger-management programs provides but a "band aid"; instead, she advocates intervention programs designed for perpetrators of domestic violence.[30]

In *Intimidades masculinas* (masculine intimacies) Latin American writer and psychologist Walter Riso presents a view of masculinity from a psychological perspective. Riso describes the emotional atrophy of many men and comments that men need to learn the "true expression of affection without using their genitals." He agrees that men in a patriarchal society need to learn how to feel. They need to have the emotional freedom to feel afraid; to feel weak; to ask for help; to fail economically; to reject aggression, war, and all types of violence; and to remain faithful to one woman.[31] It has often been noted that the web of patriarchy produces violent men (and potentially abusive women) and socializes women to be submissive.[32] Patriarchy is violent to both genders: it damages the humanity of men and undervalues the humanity of women. Since we live in a patriarchal society, we see aggression from both men and women. Conscientization training for clergy and pastoral ministers, shelters for battered women and children, and counseling to empower women are all essential.

Abusive men require special attention because they need to understand how socialization has contributed to their violent behavior. While women generally need to be empowered, men often need to be disempowered, thus creating a more equal balance of power within the family. An organization in the United States called Men Stopping Violence estimates that 50 percent of all men act violently.[33] In Latin America the percentage is likely much higher due to the more effusive emotional expression in Latin American culture and the strong emphasis on machismo in the socialization process. Nevertheless, we should not associate Latino cultures with violence; after all, violence is a learned behavior that is present to some degree in all cultures.

Batres Méndez has suggested that "to work with men means to practice a '*macho*tomy'" in order for women to regain their power and autonomy.[34] While feminists have done great work in empowering women to say no to abuse, men need help liberating themselves from the oppressive socialization they have received since birth. As feminist Florence Thomas often has said, "Women cannot do this work for men [gender analysis and awareness for change]; they need to do their own process among themselves."[35]

CHILD ABUSE

Child abuse refers to physical, psychological, social, emotional, and sexual abuse that threatens the survival, safety, self-esteem, growth and/or development of a minor. In her examination of the complex subject of power, Elizabeth Janeway says this of child abuse: "Human fathers do not eat their children, but they have certainly beaten them, starved them, misused them for their own ends and exposed them to die. Within the larger society, these family practices have been paralleled by efforts to deprive the weak of their claims on humanity."[36] While abuse obviously results from violent actions directed at children, abuse also takes the form of neglect by denying a child affection, attention, and basic needs. And a third but very significant form of abuse comes from the exposure of children to violence within the family. The degree to which family violence can produce abuse in children is clearly seen in cases where children witness and are affected by violent acts against other family members.[37]

The Federal Child Abuse Prevention and Treatment Act (42 U.S.C.A. §5106g), which originated in 1974 and has been amended several times—including by the Keeping Children and Families Safe Act of 2003—defines a minimum set of acts or behaviors that define child abuse and neglect:

- Any recent act or failure to act on the part of a parent or caretaker which results in death, serious physical or emotional harm, sexual abuse or exploitation; or
- An act or failure to act which presents an imminent risk of serious harm.

A child under this definition means a person who is under the age of eighteen or who is not an emancipated minor.[38]

According to Child Maltreatment 2005, the most recent report of data from the National Child Abuse and Neglect Data System, a division of the Department of Health and Human Services, approximately 899,000 children in this country were found to be victims of child abuse or neglect in the fiscal year 2005, a maltreatment rate of 12.1 children.[39] Casual maltreatment statistics are hard to obtain unless a child ends up in emergency care at a given hospital and a report is filed by a health-care provider of a beating, burns, broken bones, and vaginal infections or lacerations. Around the world, abuse toward children is visible in the forms of street children, child labor, children serving as soldiers, the sale of children, prostitution of children, and pornography. Another more recent and common occurrence in international child abuse has been the incorporation of children into the network of drug smuggling. It has been documented that drug smugglers use the same route to transport stolen children who are reduced to simple objects or commodities, according to the organization Casa Alianza, a division of Covenant House.[40]

Neglect, a form of child abuse, is also harmful to children. Today we have many stories of men and women who suffered neglect in their childhood, perhaps from being left home alone or even inside the car while a parent was in a bar or elsewhere. Such treatment can mark children for life, as it did an adopted member of my husband's family who, after suffering from severe neglect, was placed in foster care. Today a protective and caring mother of two children, she has vowed not to repeat the mistakes of her mother. Her brothers did not fare so well: one is in jail, and the others live unstable and difficult lives.

Dr. Miriam K. Ehrensaft, Dr. Patricia Cohen, and Jocelyn Brown led a twenty-year study investigating whether children exposed to violence between their parents have an increased risk for perpetrating violence against their partners as adults. Their study found that a history of physical abuse by caretakers appears to directly increase the possibility that a child, when an adult, will use similar ways of solving conflicts in close adult relationships. Exposure to violence between parents, which probably begins when a child is young, also seems to pose a considerable risk for becoming an adult victim of acts of partner violence. The article concludes that both males and females who were abused as children are at risk for partner violence.[41]

Child abuse has lifelong physical, psychological, behavioral, and societal consequences. It is impossible to separate these results completely. Physical consequences, such as damage to a child's growing brain, can have psychological implications, such as cognitive delay or emotional difficulties. Psychological problems often manifest themselves in high-risk behaviors. Depression and anxiety, for example, may make a person more likely to smoke, abuse alcohol or illicit drugs, or overeat. High-risk behaviors, in turn, can lead to long-term physical problems such as sexually transmitted diseases, cancer, and obesity. Abuse and neglect affect society as a whole, influencing systems of health care, education, and other human services in our communities, and they also affect the generations to come.[42]

Another result of family violence is that the abuse is reproduced; approximately half of battered wives abuse their own children. After interviewing a group of mothers in Colombia, Quintero Vásquez reported that only one-third of the mothers did *not* abuse their children, even though mothers are often aware of the potential effects of domestic violence on their children. Social workers in Colombia who interviewed women victims of domestic violence found that 47 percent of the mothers interviewed believed witnessing violent events could produce psychological disturbances in their children; 24 percent believed this violence could lead to aggressive behavior in minors. However, their awareness of the negative outcomes and their ability to prevent violent behavior from occurring are two different things altogether.[43]

Children in war-torn countries are often victimized by armed groups who either recruit children as soldiers or seize them from their homes.[44] UNICEF reports that in the armed conflicts of the 1990s one million children were orphaned or separated from their parents and ten million were psychologically traumatized. My friend José from Nicaragua was recruited when he was just fourteen. Eager to serve the cause of the revolution, José left home at night to join the battalion that was leaving the city with new and young recruits because his mother did not want him to leave. After serving over five years, he returned home with a permanent head injury. His life is now marked by constant headaches and violent nightmares that provoke violent actions.

It has been widely reported that around 300,000 children now serve as soldiers throughout the world. Most child soldiers under eighteen have been recruited into governmental armed forces, and the youngest child soldiers are about seven years old. Although the Security Council adopted the Optional Protocol prohibiting the recruitment or use of children as soldiers in 2000, the recruitment of children continues around the world.

In poverty-stricken locations, large numbers of children work on the streets, cleaning car windows or selling candy, cigarettes, fruit, phone cards, and other cheap items. This situation is common in San Salvador, Recife, Cali, and many other cities in Latin America; in Asia; and in Africa. Many street children sniff glue, inhale other chemical substances, or abuse drugs. Another serious problem is early prostitution. Mothers take twelve-year-old girls to the main square of town and charge an adult male the equivalent of US$4 for a sexual favor from the child.[45] Children displaced by war and child refugees with their families can be seen all over Sudan, Colombia, Afghanistan, and Iraq; they are fleeing from the war zones and sleeping on the streets. In some areas in Africa young girls are raped by AIDS/HIV-positive males in the belief that intercourse with a virgin will cure the disease. This myth is known as the virgin cure (it can be viewed as preventive as well) and is not unique to Africa but is found in India, Thailand, and others countries.[46] These problems have been described in *No Room at the Table: Earth's Most Vulnerable Children* and other books.[47]

Government agencies and nongovernmental organizations (NGOs) are trying to address the huge problem of children living in situations of violence. Part of their energy, in addition to providing humanitarian assistance to these children, has been focused on joining forces to work toward the creation of a climate of peace.[48] Many agencies are developing peace-education strategies, such as the Save the Children programs in Brazil, Peru, and Colombia.[49] However, the problem is enormous, and it continues to grow everywhere.

The dream of many mothers is that their daughters do not suffer as they did. This was a hope of my own mother. Her goal of continuing to attend school was crushed by my grandparents' orders that she stay home at age nine to take care of her younger siblings. However, she became a strong motivator for my sister and me. She pushed us to finish school and to go to college. She wanted to see us achieve careers and become self-supporting, independent women who would not have to depend on men. Particularly since the latter part of the twentieth century, equal educational opportunities for women have become an important part of the agenda in the United States. This has been a valid way to resist patriarchy and for mothers to equip their daughters for more promising futures. What these mothers didn't anticipate, however, was that discrimination against women and even abuse would continue to be present in the labor market, even when outlawed by federal legislation.

CARING FOR THE FAMILY

The many factors discussed above—cultural, social, economic, and psychological—form a framework for domestic abuse and also act to prevent the detection or treatment of the problem. It is important to remember that alcoholism, drug addiction, irritability, and anger are indicators of violence and not causes. They are manifestations of serious problems but never justifications for violence. Elizabeth Janeway makes this clear in her introduction to *The Power of the Weak*. She says that understanding why power is misused must be the starting point for working toward social change. Janeway maintains that the weak and oppressed need to start breaking the cycle of abuse by using "power as the ability not to please."[50]

Mennonite therapist Melissa A. Miller emphasizes that the key function of the family is to nurture its members and to care for the needs of each individual.[51] Her definition of family violence is quite broad and includes the abuse of physical, sexual, and emotional relationships and power present in the nucleus of the family.[52] She points out that when family violence exists, the concept of family changes from "safe haven" to "danger zone" for its members. Miller, a family therapist, says that to make families safe and nurturing means recognizing and ending all forms of violence in the home.

Jorge Corsi, an Argentine psychologist specializing in family violence at the University of Buenos Aires, proposes an interdisciplinary approach to the serious social problem of family violence. He uses a model that looks at the problem from a holistic perspective, considering all the different contexts within which a human being develops, without isolating or cutting the person off from his or her surroundings.[53] His model looks at three different levels—the external macro system, the exo-system, and the micro system—that interact with and affect one another. The *external macro system* includes (1) the customs and cultural values about women, men, children, and family; (2) the concepts of power and obedience; (3) attitudes on the use of force to solve problems; and (4) understandings of family roles, rights, and responsibilities. Corsi then moves to the *exo-system*, which includes (1) any legitimization of violence; (2) violent models; (3) risk factors, including stress, unemployment, social isolation, and alcoholism; (4) lack of legislation, and (5) impunity. At the final, inner level is the *micro system*, which includes (1) personal histories (violence in the family of origin); (2) learning to solve conflicts violently; (3) the use of authority in family relationships; and (4) low self-esteem and isolation.[54] Corsi's model is exemplary in the way it engages the *complexity* of family violence.

Similar to this model is the ecological model used by the WHO in its 2002 report to analyze how violence affects health; it considers violence as a product of multiple levels of influence on behavior. This model resembles the layers of an onion: individual factors are at the center, then relationships, and finally various societal factors.[55]

Quintero Vásquez suggests a similar holistic path to open up alternative solutions. She argues that although there have been different basic understandings of violence, the three models most used in approaching the problem have been the psychiatric model, the psychosocial model, and the sociocultural model. She maintains that using all three simultaneously can provide a more complete perspective on family violence.[56]

Family therapists and counselors have different ways of understanding family violence and therefore different ways of searching for viable solutions for suffering families. As a feminist, I strongly maintain that whichever approach is used must deal with the abuse of power in the family system and the overwhelming ideology of patriarchy in our society. If both lenses are not used to examine the problem, any solution proposed will be superficial and geared to a violent individual rather than to a family system that has patterns of violent behavior. The priority is to transform the male-centered structure of families but not to convert it into a female-centered system. Any system that maintains an abuse of power and control over the vulnerable within that system is wrong and needs to be transformed.

But who has the right to declare a family structure wrong, abusive, or deficient? It is generally recognized today that even if the members of the family (the insiders) are not aware of their situation of abuse, outsiders—whether the law, the community, or church members and leaders—have the right to interfere. Family violence is no longer the problem of the Miller family or the Gonzalez family, it is our problem too. We need to overcome the myth that family violence is a private matter. What happens within the walls of a home will eventually affect the schools, the churches, and the community at large.

Using an integrated or holistic approach and a feminist understanding of the misuse of power, I examine below the two cases of abuse described at the beginning of this chapter: Jessica, who was abused by her father, Julian; and Carmen, who has been abused by her violent husband, David.

The *external macro system* in which both Julian and David have been raised promotes superiority of the male over the female. In a strongly patriarchal society the defined roles of the two genders give men significant functions outside the home and women functions within the home; however, it is clearly understood that the head of the household is the husband and/or father. Julian and David are middle-aged men who grew up in a culture that comes close to consecrating the primacy of men. Their identity is based on domination and control.

They are valued if they demonstrate to the community that they are in charge of their families. Their patriarchal culture is filled with both prohibitions and prescriptions for how they are to behave and interact with others. They are prohibited from acting "like a woman"; consequently, they must not show their feelings, except for anger. They are to be "strong and tough." They may experience conflict between these cultural expectations and reality, which can produce frustration and stress. For example, how can they control the members of their families if they lack the financial resources to provide food and shelter?

The *exo-system* represented by the work place of an industrialized society reinforces role models that perpetuate the imbalance of power. Julian is fifty-two years old with a third-grade education. David, who is over sixty, grew up as a peasant and had only worked taking care of other people's farms. Their age and lack of education limit their possibilities for employment in the social and economical context of Colombia. The same is true for Jessica and Carmen. In the United States women without a high-school diploma have limited employment opportunities other than in the service industries, such as domestic work. And even with the Equal Pay Act of 1963, according to Working Women's Department AFL-CIO, women are still paid less than men when doing similar work with similar education, skills, and experience. In 1996 women were paid seventy-four cents for every dollar men received. *Maine Labor News* notes that in 2004 "women were paid 80 cents for every dollar men received."[57]

The role of father as breadwinner has been challenged by circumstances that force women to find work outside the home in order to feed the family. Tensions rise when men are left at home with the children, doing domestic work. Their self-esteem falls because the patriarchal system has taught them that they must be the breadwinner and in charge.

Corsi notes two additional factors—both of which are very significant—that contribute to higher levels of violence: a legitimization of such violence in the society and a high degree of impunity within the social system.[58] These two men have seen their own fathers fail to control their anger, spank their children violently, and batter their wives. In *On Killing: The Psychological Cost of Learning to Kill in War and Society*, Professor David Grossman, also a lieutenant colonel in the U.S. army, writes, "Through the media we are also conditioned as children and adults to kill, and when we are frightened or angry, the conditioning kicks in."[59] When these factors are stacked on top of the stress factors of poverty and unemployment, and in David's case, alcoholism, family violence is more likely to result.

The *micro system* includes the personal history of violent behavior, authoritarianism, low self-esteem, and isolation. Apparently, both Julian and David learned to solve their conflicts through violent means. The virus of violence was always present in their lives because of the patriarchal culture in which they lived. When these men attack their wives verbally or emotionally, the women, of necessity, develop mechanisms of self-defense, often including violent behavior, in resistance. But they rarely win.

More information about the two men revealed the patterns to which they had been exposed. David was raised in a Christian home with a father who had a work ethic that insisted that everyone be up at dawn to work on the farm. When the children misbehaved, his father meted out severe punishment to all. He held the Bible in his hand to demonstrate the authority given to him by God. David hated the way he and his siblings were punished by their father; he himself grew up to be a hard-working man, but one who developed a severe problem with alcohol. When angry, he repeated a similar pattern of abuse toward his children and wife.

Julian lost his father when he was only seven years old. He was raised by his mother, who was overwhelmed and frustrated trying to raise six children by herself. Julian's mother reminded him many times that he was now "the man of the house." When he was old enough, his mother demanded that he quit school and find a job to help with family expenses. Julian was expected to spank his younger siblings when they did not obey their mother. Early in life, and while still a child himself, he was given adult responsibilities and a great deal of power. He gave up his own childhood and became detached from his siblings because of his power over them, and he did what was expected of him.

According to Batres Méndez, these violent men, in their journey of socialization, have lost the capacity to feel and express pain or tenderness, especially in their relationships with women and children.[60] Amy Holtzworth-Monroe and Gregory Stuart have developed a typology of three types of male batterers. They suggest that it is important to understand differences among them in order to plan appropriate treatment and to be alert to safety concerns for the women involved. The first type (25 percent) includes men who exhibit violence only within the family. Julian, who did not fight in public but demonstrated violent behavior only toward family members, was likely this type. The second type, which includes batterers who are dysphoric (an emotional state characterized by anxiety, depression, and restlessness) or antisocial, represents another 25 percent of the batterers. David was perhaps in this second category, as he showed hostility and violence toward women inside and outside the home. Both David and Julian could benefit from treatment. This third type includes batterers who are clinically antisocial and often have criminal records. According to Holtzworth-Monroe and Stuart, such violent subtypes represent 50 percent of all batterers and are very difficult to treat or rehabilitate. They do not care if they hit their wives or children on the street, in the home of a friend, or at home. They pose a great danger to the women and children in their families and may not benefit from treatment.[61]

Based on this profile, both Julian and David have aggressive behavior. While their personalities may be seen as mild or even docile, since they are not "successful" men as defined by their society, they find and assert their identity by imposition and domination in their homes. When disobeyed or questioned, they feel their authority threatened and react with violence.

These considerations help explain David's abuse of Carmen and Julian's abuse of his daughter, Jessica. Even if David is unemployed, he still finds himself in control because he is the head of the house. He has been taught this since he was little. His father ruled the house, and everyone followed his commands. David's alcoholism adds another risk factor for his family. Access to weapons will only increase the likelihood of a serious injury to himself or his wife. Aiming a gun at Carmen's head was not only a threat but also an indication of the danger David poses to others.

Julian believes he must take care of his daughter and control her life. He distrusts her because he has been taught that children are the possessions of their parents and need someone to control them. This was what he did as the oldest of seven children. One of Julian's older sons reported that in a rage Julian once tried to strangle him. Abusers often accuse others of causing their violent behavior—"she made me angry" or "the kid raised his voice to me"—and rarely own up to their own tendencies toward violent behavior. The results are emotionally insecure children, abused wives, and in the case of Jessica, hatred and fear instead of love for her father. It is not difficult to see how such violence within a family can become self-perpetuating.

STRIVING FOR CHANGE: A HOPEFUL HORIZON

During the last two decades the feminist movement has worked to raise awareness of family violence and to change behavior patterns, not only for women but also for men. In many countries educators, psychologists, counselors, and other professionals have developed programs of gender analysis and behavior modification to meet this need. In Costa Rica, Batres Méndez provides court-mandated gender-sensitive therapy for violent men. She notes that this mandatory therapy has its limits because offenders are obligated to attend the sessions and often do not give full consent to the therapy.[62] This is also true of court-mandated treatment programs for perpetrators in this country. Obviously, offenders are more likely to change when they are willing to accept responsibility for their violent behavior and realize that they need help to change that behavior.

Gender analysis is being undertaken by men as well. The books of psychologist Walter Riso, a best-selling author in Latin America, are a meaningful resource for men struggling to become more than what the culture expects of them. Riso's *Intimidades masculinas* (masculine intimacies) calls for a new masculinity.[63] This unification of gender efforts helps men and women resist the sexist society that wants them to become collaborators in spinning the web of patriarchy. Male writers in North America in the relatively new area of masculinity and gender analysis have developed similar literature; see, for example, Robert Moore's and Douglas Gillette's *King, Warrior, Magician, Lover: Rediscovering the Archetypes of the Mature Masculine.*[64] While books alone are not going to eliminate patriarchy, they provide a vehicle to help men understand that violence is not the only way to express their masculinity.

Many countries around the world have programs to raise awareness of family violence and to bring about change. In Nicaragua, for example, a feminist organization composed of women and men, called Puntos de Encuentro (points of encounter), offers a support group for violent men that confronts them with their behavior.[65] Puntos de Encuentro studied two groups in the program, one composed of violent men and another of nonviolent men, and journeyed with them in order to better understand their makeup—why some men resort immediately to violence and why other men do not manifest the same patriarchal trail of violence. The primary finding was that the nonviolent men seemed to have support groups that affirmed and reinforced their behavior and that they were not as easily influenced by the pressure of the general culture and had learned to resist such cultural pressures.[66] Although still influenced by cultural beliefs, they were described as fish swimming against the current. They maintained their own lifestyle, even though they were seen as a minority and were subject to criticism.[67]

According to its website, No To Violence in Australia has the following goals: "to provide counselling, advisory, referral and educational services to men who have inflicted or are at risk of inflicting violence on family members and to family members exposed to male family violence or the risk of male family violence." No To Violence's programs include a counseling and referral service; training for counselors; increasing awareness of male violence in the community; facilitating networking, support, and information sharing; and undertaking research projects.

The Ohio Domestic Violence Network is a coalition that oversees and advises eighty-five county programs within the state. These programs provide crisis assistance, including basic needs such as housing, food, and clothing; referrals to community resources for health care and financial aid; emotional support and counseling; and legal services and advocacy.

The Mennonite Central Committee (MCC) sponsored a workshop on family violence in May 2001 in Akron, Pennsylvania, for Hispanic Mennonite church leaders in the United States and Canada.[68] Its title was Working Together as a Peace Church Committed to Preventing Family Violence. The workshop's objectives were to facilitate social analysis of the factors that contribute to the increase in family violence; to offer Anabaptist theological tools so church leaders can better deal with family violence theologically; and to brainstorm on how North American Latino leaders can better respond as a historic peace church to an issue Latino society struggles with daily.

The workshop posed two broad questions: Why are Latino families in North America suffering family violence? What can be done to prevent and intervene?

Carolyn Holderread Heggen, author of *Sexual Abuse in Christian Homes and Families*, gave the first presentation, which was a social analysis of the current situation. She then presented seven religious beliefs that promote abuse toward women and children.

1. It is God's will that men dominate; therefore children and women need to submit.
2. The idea that women are morally inferior to men, and that they cannot be trusted in their moral judgment, is a result of the doctrine of original sin ("The Fall").
3. To suffer is a Christian virtue, and women in particular are chosen to be "suffering servants."
4. Life in this world is hard, and we cannot expect peace and justice until we get to heaven.
5. Christians must forgive quickly; therefore women must reconcile at once with husbands who have abused them.
6. Boys and girls must obey their parents in all situations.
7. We must preserve marriage at all costs.[69]

Heggen then acknowledged that the track record of Latino churches in working to prevent family violence and to help victims recover has not been very good. Although churches make an effort to be present when there is illness in a family, they have been very cautious about responding to crises that involve violence. Heggen suggested that the role of the church should be to overcome the seven mistaken beliefs above by:

1. Teaching that men and women are equal and made in God's image.
2. Teaching that it is not appropriate for believers to use violence against anyone. Christians' model must be Jesus and his use of nonviolence, not that of the *machismo* in our society.
3. Making it the church's business when a church member uses violence, because violence in one situation affects the entire church.
4. Teaching parents how to discipline children without using violence; stating clearly in pre-marriage counseling that violence in marriage relationships is not appropriate and will not be tolerated.
5. Listening to the voices of victims and their stories to learn. Telling her story is part of the healing, and members need to celebrate with her.
6. Being sensitive when planning worship to the reality of victims present, including them in public prayers, and recognizing their pain as shared.

7. Re-examining our theology to determine how it might promote interpersonal violence. Theologians, pastors, social workers, and members need to question such teachings.
8. Committing ourselves to the ministry of walking in love with those who suffer. This is essential if we truly want to be a community of faith that promotes recovery for the hurting people among us.

A second key presenter was Irving Pérez, a Latino therapist who focuses on cultural factors in family violence. He examined the social and cultural reasons behind the abuse of women: Why do Latino men hit their mates? Why do Latina women stay in abusive relationships? He described the answer to both questions as basically the same: "Because there are sociological, psychological, economic, political, and religious conditions that permit these actions to happen with few consequences." He strongly emphasized the importance of consequences when dealing with family violence, a theme that will be addressed in a later chapter.

Pérez noted that the cognitive makeup of a Latino male dictates that when things are not going his way, he is allowed to take control by using violence. He blamed patriarchal familial structures for this sexual inequality. He spoke about the Latino population in the United States but indicated that a similar pattern exists in Latin American countries. He said that the following factors contribute to abuse in Latino families:

1. The Latino population is very diverse, both ethnically and culturally; a program of intervention for one group may not satisfy the needs of another.
2. Economically speaking, Latina women receive lower pay than men.
3. The Latino population has large family units and younger families.
4. There is a distrust of the police and the judicial system. For a Latina woman, often calling the police is like calling on an enemy for protection. Latina women desire security for themselves and their children but do not want the father of their children to be brutalized by the police.
5. Negative stereotypes like that of *machismo* and the sexy Latina enter in.

6. Latina women who come from families where there was violence look for ways to escape this cycle, but often don't succeed.[70]

Although these factors were mentioned in the context of dealing with the Latino cultures, they also hold true for non-Latino families and can come about because of other social and economic situations such as socioeconomic status, gender, ethnicity, age, alcohol or drug abuse, pregnancy, and psychiatric problems.[71]

Designing programs to address both intervention and prevention requires a multidisciplinary approach that includes full awareness of the many cultural, social, economic, and psychological factors that lead to family violence. A program must also have a clear vision of what is possible and incorporate nonviolent methods for resolving conflicts. At its heart must lie the rejection of traditional patriarchal structures. Pérez summed up the problem with these words: "This issue touches all of us in an intimate way, because all of us have been either victims, abusers, or have witnessed family violence—that is, if we have not lived on Jupiter."[72]

While there are laws in most countries that deal with family violence, including protective orders to guarantee safety to their citizens, laws in themselves are not sufficient, as is shown by the alarming statistics about family violence. Laws are an institutional step, but they are not particularly helpful for those who are trapped in abusive relationships. There is, first of all, a need to create awareness of the situations in which families are living, but also to understand that family violence is, generally speaking, a direct result of living in an androcentric, patriarchal, and hierarchical society. Unless we are able to abandon such a culture and seek dignity for both men and women, the wheel of patriarchy will continue to turn and produce violent men, submissive women, and fearful, abused, and potentially abusive children. Violence generates violence; women, men, and children living with violence can be contaminated by it.

SIGNS OF HOPE

While the situation often seems hopeless because of the strong influence of so many cultural and economic factors, there is in fact hope.

One very constructive program to bring about change and end cycles of family violence is Bridge of Hope, the vision in 1987 of two Christian women that became a reality in 1988 in Chester and Lancaster counties in Pennsylvania. It works to assist women and children in need of housing, job training, and emotional/spiritual support during a critical time in their lives. Many of these women are in their present situation because of violence within the family. Bridge of Hope partners with mentoring groups from local Christian churches who want to exemplify Christ's love to single mothers and their children who are homeless or facing eviction. After a period of training, members of the mentoring group journey with a particular family for eighteen months. They arrange housing for the family and help it connect with appropriate social-services networks. They then meet weekly with each woman and a case manager to make sure each woman is moving toward her goals. Women who successfully graduate from the program have the skills to become financially self-sufficient and have access to a support system when they need it.

In 2002, Bridge of Hope branched out to create Bridge of Hope National, a separate organization to spread the vision of churches uniting together to end and prevent homelessness for single mothers and their children. Bridge of Hope, locally and nationally, focuses on holistic, long-term solutions to poverty and homelessness. It trains and supports church-based mentoring groups in a joyful ministry of friendship with homeless families; it also provides rental assistance and professional case-management services to single mothers seeking long-term stability through job training, employment, and budgeting.[73] Although Bridge of Hope does not offer magical solutions to the complex situations of domestic violence and homelessness, over 75 percent of the women served in Lancaster and Chester counties successfully graduate with permanent housing, a circle of friends, and a plan for long-term financial self-sufficiency. During 2005 and 2006, 85 percent of the women and children served by the organization have come from situations of domestic violence, with several referrals coming directly from domestic-violence centers.

Bridge of Hope's fall 2004 newsletter tells the story of Kellie, one of the women it has assisted:

My name is Kellie and I have four children. When I was 34 years old, I found out I had breast cancer. I was advised to get a mastectomy and get chemotherapy for six months. This wasn't the worst thing, although it should have been. The worst thing was that my marriage was a complete nightmare. . . .

By the beginning of April, I realized I was dying, not from cancer, but from the monster I had married. My husband wasn't always the man he turned into and that was the deceiving part, the part that kept me hanging on to hope.

Finally, I lost all hope and realized I had to get my children and myself out of the house. But where does a mother of four children, ages 4, 5, 7, and 14, go with no job, no money and no place to feel safe? I thought I was the worst mother around. After one terrible night my oldest son said to me, "You either divorce him or I'll divorce you. Mom, we can't do this anymore." That night I promised my two boys, ages 14 and 7, that we would leave. I just needed a little time to figure out what to do.

The next day . . . my son told his best friend's mom that we were moving. She was surprised so she mentioned this to me. To my surprise I confided in her and told her the nightmare behind the facade. She then told me about Bridge of Hope. I thought it was too good to be true, but what did I have to lose? So I called them, asking for help.

A staff member explained to me that Bridge of Hope is not an emergency program and that my health issues combined with my marriage crisis was a unique situation. They told me "it's a long process." They asked me how I would financially support myself with four children and my health situation. I told them that they were talking to someone who would soon be homeless with four children and I would do whatever it took.

On June 3, 2001, after a terrible incident with my husband, my children and I left our home at 10:30 p.m. on a Sunday night. It was the last week of school and my oldest son had finals the next day. It was the first night of our long journey, but it has been a safe journey to a whole new life.

I never gave up on Bridge of Hope and evidently they never gave up on us. One day after I was living at my mom's house, they called to say they were accepting me into the program and had found a mentoring group for me. . . .

My mentors supported me by helping to furnish my house when I finally moved into my own place. They brought meals, helped my children with homework, and I even went and picked fresh vegetables from one of their gardens. Much time was spent talking over cups of coffee. One of my mentors was a graduate of Bridge of Hope herself and it was really neat to get to know her since I knew she had "been there" as well. I graduated from Bridge of Hope in August 2003 with my cancer in remission and now I'm working as a certified nursing assistant.

Bridge of Hope was our Godsend. They actually helped me hang on to hope and see great things at the end of the road. I will forever be indebted to Bridge of Hope and my mentors. A lesson I needed to learn in life was that it is okay to ask for help and in some cases absolutely necessary. Bridge of Hope allowed me to ask for help and trust in people again.

Kellie, whose name has been changed, was mentored by the Lancaster Friends Meeting.

3

Nutrients within the Trunk

Claiming a Theology of Nonviolence from Mennonite Peace Theology

After examining the nature and types of domestic violence that exist (the leaves on the tree) and the many factors that support family violence (the tree's branches), we turn now to the trunk of the tree. The trunk channels to the leaves and branches both nutrients and contaminants gathered from the soil by the roots. In particular, we will focus on the religious beliefs that have allowed the perpetuation of violence. Unfortunately, our Christian churches have often been complicit in this process and must bear some responsibility for it. While we hold the church accountable, we must also recognize the good that has been accomplished, particularly as church leaders seek better understanding of the complex arena of family violence and training to be able to assist its victims.

A VOICELESS VOICE, STILL IN THE MARGIN

My aunt's story is sad, like the stories of so many women who suffer from family violence. Isabel married early to escape from the poverty of her parents' home. Her two brothers described her as someone who always wanted the best and was very proud of the dresses she sewed. When it was time to marry, she chose the most eligible man in her neighborhood, a soldier who had just returned from the Korean

War and looked very elegant in his uniform. Their courtship was short, and, since he was well known in the neighborhood, they soon were married. Their wedding day was a dream—Isabel in a white bridal gown and veil and her groom in his uniform.

He quickly found a job at the prison as a security guard, and Isabel stayed at home having baby after baby. She spent most of her days alone in their simple wooden house on the hill. He usually came home late from work. Most evenings he went to the local Pentecostal church where he had given his life to Christ. He prayed hard and harassed Isabel even harder to join his church, but she was not interested. She had her own religion, that which her parents believed in and practiced. He, however, viewed his wife's beliefs as demonic ideas that would take her straight to hell. In the beginning, she had shouted back at him but over the years she became more withdrawn. She could never deny him sex except when she had her period.

At the end of her tenth pregnancy, her youngest brother noticed an enormous growth in her belly that was not part of her eight-month pregnancy. He spoke to her husband, demanding that his sister receive medical treatment for this growth right after the baby was born. He also advocated sterilization for Isabel because of her poor health. Her living conditions were not suited for more children, and her mental health was steadily deteriorating.

After the baby was born, her brother visited to confirm that the operations, including sterilization, had been done. At this point in her life, Isabel was not talking much. Feeling pity, he asked to pray for her, placing a bible on her bed. In silence and as an act of rebellion and anger, Isabel threw the bible as far away as her strength allowed. Her action said more than words. I interpreted her silence and action as saying, "I don't want anything to do with this Bible, this faith, this religion." Although the intentions of her brother, who had started attending a charismatic Catholic church, were well intended, they were not well received by Isabel. She had been abused sexually, emotionally, and religiously by her Christian husband and perhaps held the church responsible for her situation.

As a survival mechanism, she took on the robe of silence, speaking to no one. Even today, several years after the death of her husband, her niece visits her, whispering in her ear: "You can talk now. He is dead." But Isabel had died to life a long time before her husband. The truth lay in her silence, which grew from abuse in the name of God, in the name of the religious beliefs of her husband. Her tree of life was contaminated by the nutrients of religious and social submission.

The goal of this chapter is to explore more closely the tools of peace theology and how peace theology can be used to stop family violence. By tools I mean those biblical teachings understood by the peace churches as the core beliefs of our tradition. They include true discipleship and the peaceful values of the kingdom of God and the church, theological concepts that can help us as Christian churches to overcome family violence. In order to reclaim the theology of nonviolence, it is essential to review the Anabaptist heritage of Mennonite peace theology in North America, including its strengths and limitations as a theology of peace and how it has been applied over time. Following this brief history of the Mennonite tradition, I examine three biblical beliefs that seem to have been misinterpreted and misused in ways that undermine the role of women and lead to the perpetuation of family abuse: the understanding of the cross, the understanding of suffering, and the concept of church. In questioning these theological concepts, I reconstruct some biblical teachings from a feminist perspective, focusing on Matthew 5:38–39, the portion of the Sermon of the Mount that refers to turning the other cheek. This text has often been misinterpreted and misused in ways that promote abuse. In addition to looking for pitfalls such as this, it is also important to scrutinize individual texts to determine if they are in harmony with the teaching of Jesus as a nonviolent model for our lives.

THE ANABAPTIST MOVEMENT

Discussing peace theology without mentioning the Anabaptist movement of the sixteenth century would be like a daughter not recognizing the mother that gave her birth. Those radical Christians of the sixteenth century were called Anabaptists because of their practice of adult baptism; becoming an Anabaptist meant being baptized or rebaptized. The Anabaptists, in contrast with the reformers, theologians, and preachers who were their contemporaries, were not known for their theological writings. Although Conrad Grebel, Menno Simons, Melchior Hofmann, Pilgram Marpeck, and Michael Sattler, among others, did leave behind some important writings, the Anabaptist preachers were known primarily for practicing their faith by rescuing the teachings of Jesus in the gospels. Their writings were principally pastoral letters to the believer church movement of their time.

Similar to reformers such as Martin Luther and Ulrich Zwingli, the Anabaptists denounced the way in which Christianity had lost its truth and direction and the close relationship that had grown between church and state. The established religion, Roman Catholicism, resisted change and sought to maintain its power. The Anabaptists quickly gained many enemies; in addition to the Catholic leaders and governments, Reformation Protestants felt threatened by the radical way in which Anabaptist Christians were teaching and living out Jesus' words in the gospel narratives. These early Anabaptists chose a simple lifestyle separated from the world's kingdom, obeying only the rule of God. Cruel persecution drove them from the major cities to the countryside of northern Europe. Many became martyrs.

Menno Simons, from Holland, left the Catholic priesthood in 1536 and joined the Anabaptist movement. He became the leader of the Anabaptists in the Netherlands, and his followers were called Mennists or Mennonites. Menno was a simple priest whose writings were pastoral letters to the movement's followers.

Mennonite theological reflections can be found in the Schleitheim Confession of Faith of 1527 and hymnals, among other writings.[1] The early leaders intentionally shied away from writing theological pieces that would be "more paper and less practice." The theology of our foremothers and forefathers (called at the time by some "the theology of the road") of the sixteenth century is thus written in the lives of the thousands of Anabaptists who were killed or who survived the persecution for living and sharing a radical Christ-centered faith.[2] It is interesting to note that the theology of the road has become an attractive concept and practice in the last twenty-five years for Latin American Anabaptist Mennonite theologians, who have made a connection between Anabaptist theology and liberation theology. The theology of the road refers to the ongoing process of people who live the word of God while being surrounded by suffering and injustice, but who still maintain hope.

The way of love and nonresistance as portrayed in the New Testament has characterized the Anabaptist movement from the beginning. Even in the sixteenth century Menno Simons wrote about the importance of Christians not participating in warfare: "The regenerated do not go to war," he stated, adding that they are the children of peace, who have beaten their swords into plowshares and their spears into pruning hooks, and know of no war. Conrad Grebel, one of the first Swiss Anabaptist leaders, said, "True, believing Christians neither use the worldly sword nor engage in war since, among them, taking human life has ceased entirely, for we are no longer under the old covenant."[3]

Mennonite historian C. Arnold Snyder takes us back to the core of Anabaptist thinking and living by acknowledging the diverse pacifist stances of several groups. All the strands were present in the first-generation Anabaptists, from Thomas Munster's involvement with the Revolt of the Peasants in 1525 to Menno Simons's focus on nonresistance. "All had in common the yielding to Christ that enabled the Anabaptists to act in love even in situations of violence."[4]

THE MENNONITES IN NORTH AMERICA

The theology of nonresistance from early Anabaptist history is the forebear of today's theology of nonviolence. This belief was the primary reason that Mennonites migrated to the United States, first settling in Germantown, Pennsylvania, in 1683. One cause of the European Mennonite migration to North America was the obligatory military service imposed by Napoleon early in the seventeenth century. The early Anabaptists took their theology of nonresistance from the text of Matthew 5:39: "Do not resist one who is evil." Primarily understood as not harming anyone or not using force to protect oneself, it taught a self-sacrificial attitude through imitation of Christ. This faith belief was expressed in conscientious objection to serving in war. Historically, however, the Mennonites did compromise by providing a substitute or paying a fine for not going to war. They also practiced nonresistance by not seeking retribution or punishment for those who harmed them.[5]

After their migration to America, the Mennonites who settled in Pennsylvania were united against military service and in favor of giving relief to the suffering. Guy Franklin Hershberger writes: "War is always a trying experience for nonresistant people. In such a time there is naturally a temptation to compromise one's faith."[6] During times of war Mennonites have searched for creative ways to keep the faith and hold to their beliefs. For example, in 1742 they published the Mennonite hymnbook, *Ausbund*, which contained many stories of Anabaptists who suffered for their nonresistance, and in 1748 they published a new German version of the *Martyrs Mirror*, an account of the Anabaptist martyrs of the sixteenth century.[7]

During the American Civil War some young members of the church joined the military, arousing the church and producing a revival of the teaching on nonresistance and a great awakening in the Mennonite churches.[8] In June 1863 John F. Funk encouraged Mennonite Bishop John M. Brenneman from Allen County to publish his well-known book *Christianity and War*. Funk later produced a booklet titled *Warfare, Its Evil, Our Duty*. These two documents were products of the urgency of the times and represented the diverse ways in which Mennonites and other pacifist groups were seeking a way to address the Civil War. The subtitle of Funk's book is *Addressed to the Mennonite churches throughout the United States, and all others who sincerely seek and love the truth*. The motif of the book is to offer the "truth" to the churches that had abandoned their identity of nonresistance.

In 1917 the Mennonites faced their hardest test to date: obligatory conscription during World War I. Because of their beliefs, over two thousand Mennonite men were sent to prison camps. In World War II, 40 percent of the volunteer conscientious objectors in the United States who served in the Civilian Public Service were Mennonites.[9]

In response to World War II and the Korean Conflict, the 1940s and 1950s saw the publication of several major works written to recover the historical and theological identity of North American Mennonites. One was "The Anabaptist Vision," a keynote speech given by Harold S. Bender in December 1943 to the American Society of Church History and later published in the *Mennonite Quarterly Review*.[10] Bender offered a contemporary historical reflection on Anabaptist identity. Guy Franklin Hershberger was the author of another work, *War, Peace, and Nonresistance*, a theological and biblical reflection on the theology of nonresistance published in 1953. These two works, along with J. C. Wenger's *Discipleship*,[11] were noteworthy efforts from a North American Mennonite perspective to guide the twentieth-century church back to its Anabaptist roots. Bender's "Anabaptist Vision" and Hershberger's Mennonite ideal of community and discipleship both served as models for revitalization. And in 1954 Elizabeth Hershberger Bauman published *Coals of Fire*, a children's book of fascinating faith stories illustrating the courage of those who took a stand for nonresistance and peace.[12]

After 1949 a renewal of interest in peace and nonresistance took place among French, German, Swiss, and North American Mennonites.

By 1950, Mennonite voices were being heard outside their own circles as they contributed to worldwide discussions on peace. A call arose for all Mennonites to fulfill the task entrusted to us by our Anabaptist forbears and join in the propagation of the gospel of peace. Mennonite mission boards and the Peace Section of the MCC began to promote a witness for peace in Mennonite churches in India, Indonesia, Africa, and South America, particularly in Argentina, Uruguay, and Brazil.[13]

Alternative service programs for conscientious objectors took Mennonites into Puerto Rico, the country of my birth; the conscientious objectors provided medical care for the poor. In 1947 the first Mennonite church in Puerto Rico began in conjunction with the Mennonite hospital in La Plata, Puerto Rico, which today is one of the best private hospitals located in the center of the island.

Toward a Theology of Nonviolence:
The Movements of the 1960s and 1970s

In the 1960s the Vietnam War pushed Mennonites to go beyond making pronouncements against war. Mennonites began sending people to serve on relief assignments and to be a presence with the victims of the war. This was a turning point, as Mennonite theologians started writing about the theology of peace and social action, and naming the injustices of people living in the war zones. The MCC sponsored these volunteers.

The emerging theology of peace gained strength during the Vietnam War. Peace church theologians who returned from serving overseas had been touched by a different reality and strongly moved by political and social injustice. Back home, the feminist and civil rights movements also influenced the Mennonite Church, causing Mennonites to question some of their beliefs and question how to bring about peace in this world.

During the 1960s and 1970s, when the civil rights movement and the Vietnam War occupied American minds and churches, several Mennonite leaders and Mennonite-related individuals began to shift theological and ethical discussions away from the centrist doctrine on nonresistance to war. Sociologist Cal Redekop opened discussions about the faithfulness of the church during times of war. The world's events fomented new thoughts among Mennonite theologians, and

nationally the struggle for civil rights affected theologians of all traditions. Theologian-philosopher-ethicists J. R. Burkholder and J.
Lawrence Burkholder began rethinking the Mennonite doctrine of
nonviolent resistance.

During his leadership directing (with his wife, Rosemarie) the
Mennonite House in Atlanta, Georgia, from 1961 to 1964, black historian and theologian Vincent Harding insisted that the church asser-
tively confront racism and segregation. Dr. Harding was instrumental
in moving the leaders of the denomination to become more involved
in the civil rights struggle, better known in the south as the Southern
freedom movement. White Mennonites still recall with emotion the
first time they marched in Washington to support the primary issues
raised by the movement. Later on, discouraged, Dr. Harding and his
wife decided not to return to the Mennonite House because of differences with the leadership.

During the 1960s and 1970s issues of gender raised by women also
influenced Mennonites. At Goshen College, a Mennonite college in
Indiana, several Mennonite women (including Dorothy Yoder Nyce,
a professor of scripture; Anna Bowman, chair of the social work department; campus pastor Diane MacDonald; and director of student
services Ruth Krall) raised the "woman question" as a necessary aspect of Mennonite peace theology. Mennonite feminists began to play
a role in shaping the minds and lives of young men and women.

In the 1980s Mennonite volunteers in Central America became involved in working for peace. They walked alongside other Christians
resisting violence and experienced the heavy burden of sadness and
anger at the murder of Archbishop Oscar Romero of El Salvador on
March 24, 1980, and at the deaths of many more innocent victims.
Everyone cried for justice saying, "¡No más muerte! (no more death)."

By the end of the twentieth century the conviction had grown within
the Mennonite Church that the way of peace was an integral part of
the gospel of Christ. While the group struggling with justice-and-
peace issues was small, as Beulah Stauffer Hostetler pointed out, it
forcefully questioned the relevance of Christian pacifism in relation
to social responsibility.[14]

Although pacifism is a biblical concept, until the late 1960s Mennonite theologian Guy Franklin Hershberger still found it difficult to
abandon the word *nonresistance*, although he recognized that many people
preferred the word *pacifism* because it was positive, as opposed to the
negative connotations of *nonresistance*. The traditional Mennonite

belief was that *nonresistance* described the faith and life of those who accept scripture as the will of God and will not take part in warfare.[15] Mennonite theologians such as Hershberger were concerned that *pacifism* could possibly involve coercive action, leading to more violence. Considerable discussion took place about the meaning of nonviolence versus nonresistance. Hershberger stated that nonresistance is first of all about loving and obeying God, with a strong emphasis on love among the fellowship of believers. Nevertheless, both understandings of peace believe that one must not respond to evil with the tools of evil. Perhaps one could say that Mennonite writers, such as H. S. Bender, J. C. Wenger, and Hershberger, moved by the events of their times but still holding dear the belief of "do not resist," were trying to reclaim their understanding of the gospel of peace.

Mennonite leaders who wanted the church to become more active in its peace stance reflected that while Mennonites might know how to be peaceable, they make weak peacemakers when their nonresistance becomes noninvolvement.[16] As Mennonite awareness of events and issues both at home and abroad increased, it resulted in more active stands of nonviolence. Hostetler notes that Mennonites made major contributions to peace theology during the 1980s, such as the writings of John Howard Yoder. Mennonite scholars became a major source of creative nonviolent theology and biblical analysis and were read by a much broader audience than Mennonites.[17] Historically, nonresistance formed part of the theology of war Mennonites used to counter the specific evil of war, and violence was described in terms of war and weapons.[18] When the term *nonviolence* began to erupt in the 1970s, it was necessary to define violence more broadly in order to include other expressions of covert violence, such as political and social injustice and institutional violence.

By the mid-twentieth century Mennonite theologians interpreted *nonresistance* literally as being passive to any attack so as to do no violence to the attacker. On the other hand, *nonviolence*, particularly as it is used today by third-world theologians, is a more contextualized interpretation of the gospel of peace; it calls for an active stance in solving a given situation. Nonresistance requires a passive position toward injustice, while nonviolence requires an active restorative process to work toward justice and peace.

Adherents to the more conservative perspective understand the world with a "two-kingdom theology," an Anabaptist teaching formulated in the Schleitheim Confession of 1527, the first Anabaptist confession of faith.[19] It was based on the biblical presentation of heaven and hell in which heaven, or the kingdom of God, is the goal of the believer who takes on the discipline of discipleship in order to become worthy of that kingdom. This was interpreted by Mennonites as a reason to withdraw from the world.[20] Thus, when European Mennonites arrived in the New World, they largely kept themselves separate from it. The church of the brotherhood and sisterhood, the *Gemeindeschaft*, was an attempt to put the two-kingdom belief into practice in everyday living. Mennonites by then were known not by their theology but rather by their ethical lives. Communities withdrew to remote places such as Moravia and Russia in Europe, the Great Plains of North America, and Paraguay in South America. These Anabaptist Mennonites suffered much, but they lived as they believed the gospel of Jesus was calling them to do.[21] This unworldly but hopeful life in community and simple living re-created the kingdom values here on earth. It must be noted, however, that these values were patriarchal in nature and strongly favored men over women.

A theology of nonviolence was also emerging in many Christian-based communities in Latin America, and there were similarities between liberation theology and the Mennonite theology of peace. Because of their theological position, Mennonites did not engage in any forms of violence, but they did raise prophetic voices to denounce the injustices their brothers and sisters in Central American were suffering as a result of U.S. Cold War strategies in the region. The emerging biblical theology of nonviolence was once again a product of seeing war and saying no to its tactics and of desiring to work for justice by refraining from harming others.

From War Theology to a Theology of Nonviolence

In the late 1940s and through the 1950s, many sociopolitical events touched Mennonites in the United States. World War II, with its challenges to a peace stance on non-involvement in war, had hit the Mennonite community hard. Several Mennonite youth did enroll as soldiers in those wars because their churches were not strong advocates of conscientious objection, a position that had developed as a response to practices of nonresistance (although some Mennonite men did claim conscientious objector status). But in the 1960s Mennonites who came of age during the Vietnam War were educated and involved in social activism outside of their religious communities. The civil rights movement, large and violent demonstrations in major cities, and the assassinations of Martin Luther King, Jr., President Kennedy, and Attorney General Robert Kennedy all contributed to the foment for action in the name of peace.

The theology of nonresistance seemed to be evolving in the direction of activist nonviolent work and writings. One such program of the MCC was PAX (1950–76) in which participants did manual labor to help rebuild Europe. Participants included activists. For example, Mennonite Church witnesses Earl and Pat Hostetler Martin and Doug Hostetler went to Vietnam to work with refugees. From the beginning, Doug pushed the MCC for a more activist approach in its refugee work. When the American troops were pulled out of Vietnam, American Mennonite service workers also left, with the exception of MCC staff member Earl Martin, who chose to stay behind to witness to the power of nonviolent love.

It is important to note that during this time the majority in the Mennonite Church supported the concept of nonresistance while just a few leaders, theologians, anthropologists, sociologists, and historians voiced active nonviolent positions. Many who had done most of their graduate work outside the Mennonite world as doctoral students at Harvard and Princeton and in Chicago and Amsterdam were now contributing to the peace discussions.

The Women's Movement

Another form of social change that affected Mennonites, and particularly women, was the women's movement of the mid-twentieth century. As a result, a program in women's biblical theology was initiated at Goshen College in the 1970s, when campus pastor Diane MacDonald and her husband, Dennis, taught a course entitled "The Bible and Sexuality." After the MacDonalds left, Dorothy Yoder Nyce continued teaching the course. For the first time, these faculty members "applied a feminist perspective in a biblical interpretation class" at Goshen.[22] Several years later (1985–86), feminist theologian and psychotherapist Ruth Krall began to teach feminist analysis in her religion courses. By fall 1986 Krall was named program director of the campus peace-studies program. In this role a feminist voice was brought to the center of peace studies. This meant a feminist critique of war and an analysis of sexual violence—including domestic violence—were addressed.

In the 1980s Dorothy Yoder Nyce helped the MCC open a Women's Concerns desk, and in 1986 the MCC asked Krall to visit churches to talk about domestic violence and professional abuse. The Associated Mennonite Biblical Seminaries held a consultation in October 1991 to bring together persons within the peace-church tradition who had dealt with the topic of violence against women and peace theology and to encourage further work on these issues.[23] According to Krall, what really dampened the progress of the issues of women's abuse that were emerging within the Mennonite churches was the accusation of sexual misconduct of widely known Mennonite theologian John Howard Yoder. The voices of outspoken women leaders like Ruth Krall and Carolyn Holderread Heggen were marginalized, and personal criticism was even raised, intended to silence them.

Because of all these events, and particularly the war in Vietnam, the struggles of the poor in Latin America, and the women's movement, the question "Who are we as Mennonites?" was open for debate; prophetic voices, although not large in number, kept the issue of peace alive. The emergence of these demonstrations for peace was in the hands of key Mennonite activists who no longer spoke of a theology of *nonresistance* but of a theology of *nonviolence*. Mennonites in war zones were denouncing U.S. policy rather than fighting. They were no longer passive; on the contrary, they were people active in the face of conflict, whether for issues of war, social injustice, gender discrimination, or racism. Instead of just talking about what was wrong, these were people willing to work for change.

THE SHORTCOMINGS OF THE NONVIOLENCE MOVEMENT

It is difficult but essential work to be a beacon of light and hope in the midst of a sea of violence. Unfortunately, however, the light of active nonviolence that was aimed at broader social issues did not reach into family life. The personal lives of many of the activist leaders revealed a dichotomy of practices and beliefs. It seemed easier to talk and work for peace outside the home than inside. Known for their church's advocacy of peace and justice, Mennonite leaders initiated practices of religious freedom and tolerance of conscience for men who did not want to serve in wars. However, such peacemaking efforts failed to be applied in their homes. Do we continue to see the world as two divided kingdoms, not the kingdoms of heaven and hell, but those of public life and private life?

We live in a world in which we are called to proclaim and give witness to God's peace. Anabaptism has always been sourced in the biblical tradition known as community hermeneutics, when the faithful come together as a congregation to interpret the Bible. The final word does not come from the pastor but from the community. The community of faith is in dialogue with scripture and is allowed to question the texts. Through this communal exercise, we search for discernment of God's will with one another. This practice was followed back in the sixteenth century when, while questioning baptismal practices, communities of Christians, after serious reflection, understood adult baptism as a biblical mandate. In more recent times, again influenced heavily by scripture, Mennonites have shown partiality toward those who suffer and feel compelled to denounce injustices.[24]

Anabaptists are all over the world today, still interpreting the gospel of peace in the Bible and being shaped by its message. The essential core of Anabaptist beliefs continues to be an understanding of Jesus as a peacemaker. The Anabaptist "theology on the road"[25] is still valid today as Anabaptist theology is reshaped by new influences. Similarly, the women's movement has influenced the theology of nonviolence. Feminist perspectives have shed light on nonviolence as not just another theological teaching but as a way of living in harmony with all. Some Mennonite feminists, such as myself, are working to eliminate violence by overturning patterns of socialization that make use of violence. A faith community advocating a gospel of peace should work against violence in all the systems that support life, including the church itself.

Nonviolence is powerful, Richard Gregg states in *The Power of Nonviolence*, first published in 1934. In a later edition (1959) he writes that "nonviolence does not break the opponent's will but alters it, does not destroy the opponent's confidence . . . but transfers [it] to a finer purpose."[26] After traveling to India and studying Gandhi's method of nonviolence and its results, Gregg was convinced of the power of nonviolence and its benefit for humanity. The power of nonviolence will work if we practice it and discover its usefulness in disarming violence. Counter-cultural in nature, nonviolence is a profound spiritual practice that can provide a guide for living, particularly if put into practice in our relationship with our children, spouses, and other people we come in contact with. Practicing nonviolence means treating others with dignity and never perpetuating abusive behavior. It comes from a profound conviction that violence is not a viable solution.

WORKING WITH A FEMINIST PERSPECTIVE ON SCRIPTURE

In the words of New Testament scholar Sharon H. Ringe:

> The Bible *is* a powerful book. Because of that power, the question of interpretation goes beyond merely understanding the Bible, to ask also, having understood it as best we can, what is its force in our lives and what are we to do with or about it? The question is not an easy one, especially for women. In the first place, the power of the Bible in women's lives has been at best ambivalent. It has functioned as a force for life, for hope, and for liberation. . . .
>
> At the same time, women reading the Bible have found themselves on alien and even hostile turf. Rarely if ever do women in the Bible get to speak for themselves. Rather, they are portrayed from the perspective of male authors and in the context of religious communities where authority finally came to be vested in men and where men's experience was the norm.[27]

We need to struggle with the texts, just as Jacob struggled with the angel, to understand the meaning of the passages in our context and to interpret these texts in an appropriate manner. My woman's eyes and heart may see, feel, and understand the texts differently than male theologians or exegetes. The text themselves can then become liberating for the church and our families and can serve as valuable tools for teaching and for counteracting interpretations harmful to women and families.

A biblical text that is key to the Anabaptist understanding of resisting violence is Matthew 5:38–39: "You have heard that it was said, 'An eye for an eye and a tooth for a tooth.' But I say to you, Do not resist an evildoer. But if anyone strikes you on the right cheek, turn the other also." Much confusion and many contradictions have arisen through varying interpretations of this text, which I intend to look at closely from a feminist perspective using an approach called a feminist hermeneutic of suspicion. This approach, with the goal of reconstructing the truth behind the text, is particularly helpful in understanding texts written in a patriarchal tradition. It looks beyond the written words to rescue a non-sexist meaning whenever possible.[28]

Looking at the Text

The New Revised Standard Version entitles the beginning of this section "Concerning Retaliation." The verses are part of the larger text (Mt 5:3—7:27) known as the Sermon on the Mount, a text that focuses on the values of *basileia*, the kin-dom of God, and includes the familiar Beatitudes and the admonitions to become the "salt of the earth" and the "light of the world." Beginning with 5:38, Jesus spoke to his disciples against the old Law, which permitted retaliation for received offenses (Ex 21:24; Lv 24:20; Dt 19:21). While it seems that Jesus might have been trying to decrease violence, the example he used—"if anyone strikes you on the right cheek, turn the other"— seems to provoke the oppressor to more violence. To what group in Jewish society, with its clear social classifications, was Jesus referring? Who had the right to hit another person on the cheek in public? A blow to the cheek was certainly a personal offense, particularly in a public setting, according to Walter Wink.[29]

The *lex talionis*, the law of equal retribution, served a twofold purpose: it upheld the right of the injured one to seek retribution, and it limited the extent of retaliation. The crowd gathered before Jesus was hearing a new law: "Do not retaliate or use your [law-given] rights." In his commentary on Matthew, Richard Gardner suggests this was a call to find new ways of responding to injury.[30] The action to strike was regulated by a law that allowed the owner of a slave to strike on the cheek in public only once to correct the slave's behavior. Striking the offender more than once would be considered abusive. Masters backhanded slaves, husbands did the same with their wives, parents did this with their children. And Romans treated Jews in this way, says Walter Wink. He reminds us that the action itself demonstrated unequal relations and thus was an issue of power. To resist, Wink says, means neither to submit nor to assault. Instead, Wink suggests it aims at a way to "secure your human dignity and begin to change the power equation."[31]

The crowd that may have gathered to listen to Jesus address his disciples is presumed to have comprised people who were subject to the dehumanizing treatments of a hierarchical system of class, race, gender, age, and status.[32] They heard Jesus tell them that slaves should allow themselves to be struck twice, which would be a shameful public exposure for the owner. Wink suggests that what we are dealing with here is insult—the intention is to humiliate, not to start a fistfight.[33] Perhaps Jesus was suggesting a third way, a strategy that would expose the cruel injustice of the system itself. But while turning the other cheek was a cultural expression with particular meaning in the Judeo-Gentile context of that time, does it have meaning today in our context? Might it be pertinent to our concerns with family violence?

In his commentary *Matthew and the Margins: A Sociopolitical and Religious Reading*, Warren Carter maintains that Jesus is advocating "active nonviolent resistance." He points out that a more accurate translation of the Greek text of Matthew 5:39a is "Do not violently resist an evildoer" instead of "Do not resist an evildoer."[34] Carter notes that it would be "strange indeed" for Jesus to advocate violence in these verses: "Since [Matthew] 5:21, four scenes have exhorted the audience to resist doing evil!" Carter argues that since Jesus resisted evil many times during his life (including resisting the devil in 4:1–11), Jesus is instructing his disciples in a way of "resisting oppressive powers."[35] To give the other "cheek" means not being controlled by or submitting to the violence of the other. Carter concludes:

> Rather than be subdued into nonresponsiveness, and rather than lashing out in violence and continuing the cycle, Jesus teaches a third response: *turn the other also*. This action shows that one has not been intimidated or provoked into uncontrolled actions. It is a chosen, active, nonviolent response to a system designed to humiliate. The chosen action refuses submission, asserts dignity and humanness, and challenges what is supposed to demean. It refuses the superior the power to humiliate.[36]

And this is a beginning in breaking the cycle of violence.

An Anabaptist Reading of the Text

The Anabaptists of the sixteenth century interpreted the Sermon on the Mount as the mandated law of God.[37] These teachings of Jesus illustrated the way a Christian life must be lived. According to its "rule of love," the Anabaptist community of faith interpreted Matthew 5:38–39 as a call to love one's enemy rather than to seek revenge.[38] In *Siguiendo a Jesus: Comentario sobre el Sermon del Monte, Mateo 5* (following Jesus, commentary on the Sermon of the Mount, Matthew 5), Mennonite Juan Driver notes that Jesus' teaching to respond without violence was new and revolutionary. The four examples Jesus uses of how to respond to violence—giving your coat and your cloak, walking a second mile, giving to those who beg and not refusing to lend, and turning the other cheek—must not be used in a legalistic way, but serve as examples to explain the teaching. According to Driver, these examples are methods that interrupt the spiral of violence.[39]

In *Jesus y la no Violencia* (Jesus and nonviolence), Dionisio Byler reminds us that violence does not originate from God but from a profound rejection of God and of God's purpose in creating humankind.[40] The right to denounce injustice committed toward women is rooted in the power to denounce all violence and instead announce the gospel of peace.

The Text and Family Violence

I feel a difficult struggle within me as I read this passage: How should I counsel a battered woman who has been hit by her husband? Is this passage implying that she should stay in this abusive situation, knowing that she will be hit again? Yet striking back will only nurture the circle of violence, causing more hurt and probably exposing a woman or a child to more physical violence. In his struggle for justice, Martin Luther King, Jr., said on May 3, 1963, "The old law of an eye for an eye leaves everybody blind."[41] The same principle applies for women who turn the other cheek: they have given their other cheek too many times already, and the abusers have not been confronted. A safe way to expose the abuser is to empower the abused woman to leave the home. As a public manifestation that the woman will no longer tolerate the abuse, such an action could have the power of "giving the other cheek."

Although the text of Matthew 5:38–39 has often been used to admonish wives, this was not its intent. Jesus was telling slave owners not to abuse their power by mistreating their slaves. Church leaders, and all people of good will, must understand that while the Gospel of

Matthew does include texts that refer to husbands and wives (for example, Matthew 5:31–32 on divorce), Matthew 5:38–39 is not directed to these relationships. Indeed, Matthew 5:31–32 includes an implicit teaching to consider the wife and not abandon her for any false reasons. Matthew 5:37–38 certainly does not apply to women being abused by their partners; it was a mandate, instead, to control the abuse of slaves by their owners. While the patriarchal nature of scripture rarely provided for women, we need to trust in the loving nature of Jesus; he would not have allowed for the abuse of women by their husbands.

Richard Gardner describes Jesus as redefining the law and even surpassing the Old Testament Law with a law of love.[42] The Anabaptists held that the word of Jesus should govern conduct in social relationships as well. Menno Simons asked, "How can a Christian then defend war, violence, stealing, slaying, etc.?"[43] To this, we could add, How can we accept the actions of a Christian husband who abuses his wife or children? We need a different model. We need our church members to search together to find new Christlike ways to overcome the violence in their lives.

CONNECTIONS BETWEEN THE TEACHINGS IN SCRIPTURE AND FAMILY VIOLENCE

Chapters 1 and 2 of this book describe in some detail the leaves and branches of the tree called family violence and identify significant factors such as the influence of patriarchy and gender-role differences, as well as the socioeconomic factors and psychological/emotional dimensions that can be present. For Christian families, there are often theological and biblical interpretations that influence the tree of family violence, poisoning it or providing rich nutrients that lead to healing. I believe three theological understandings are key: the way we view the cross, the way we interpret the role of suffering, and the way we understand church.

Questioning the Theology of the Cross

It is important to recognize that not all Christian feminists understand the theology of the cross in the same way. Some theologians, including Joanne Carlson Brown and Rebecca Parker, have abandoned atonement theology as a load that is too heavy to carry, while others are seeking to renew the meaning of the symbol of the cross, including the concept of suffering, in order to understand how the church can give new hope to victims. From the perspective of Brown and Parker, atonement theology seems rooted in violence, namely, the killing of Jesus. The classic atonement doctrine presents the image of "divine child abuse" and serves as a model that encourages women to submit passively to abuse. Their opinion is that a "Christian theology with atonement at the center still encourages martyrdom and victimization."[44] Consequently, some feminist and womanist voices have challenged the belief that the death of Jesus resulted from a divine need for justice.[45]

Going a step further, Mennonite professor J. Denny Weaver questions a "Christendom that claims salvation via the death of Christ on the grounds that it accommodates violence and the sword."[46] Weaver argues that atonement theory needs to be interpreted differently, that it needs to go back to the life of Jesus in the gospels, including the testimony left behind by the emerging church of the first century. Weaver proposes a "narrative *Christus Victor*," in contrast to Gustaf Aulén's classical *Christus Victor*.[47] Weaver's narrative *Christus Victor* is a way of reading the entire history of God's people with the life, death, and resurrection of Jesus as the culminating revelation of the reign of God in history. In Weaver's interpretation, the death of Jesus is clearly the work of the forces of evil. It was not something that God needed or intended. Jesus' mission was to make visible the reign of God, and his suffering and death were the result of opposing evil.[48] Weaver's narrative *Christus Victor* is an atonement model that turns passive victims into responsible actors in the history of salvation. In summary, Weaver's work focuses on the life of Jesus, not on his death, and it is this life that provides a model for nonviolence.

While there is no universal agreement among feminist theologians about the redemptive nature of the suffering and death of Jesus, there is a growing consensus that the issue is critical to emerging theologies that seek to overcome violence against women and children. Rosemary Radford Ruether explains that suffering is the risk one takes when struggling to overcome unjust systems whose beneficiaries resist change. Redemption then comes through conversion.[49] Brown and Parker believe that Jesus' death was overcome by the resurrection, that Jesus refused to submit to the threat of death. By walking out of the tomb, he refused to abandon his commitment to the truth.[50]

Of all the symbols in the history of Christendom, the choice of the cross for strong emphasis has been oppressive for women suffering abuse from their husbands. Even today many church leaders are telling women they must "carry their cross" and stay in abusive relationships. But the cross represents death and pain. In dealing with this emphasis, like many other feminists, I am struggling for an appropriate meaning of the cross for us today. Was death necessary for salvation? In searching for a renewed Anabaptist meaning of the theology of the atonement, I have found the research and writings of Juan Driver and J. Denny Weaver very helpful.

In *Understanding the Atonement for the Mission of the Church*, Driver describes two key historical moments in the development of a theology of atonement, the understanding that the death of Jesus was essential for salvation.[51] The first was created by Paul, who borrowed the symbol of atonement from the practice of animal sacrifice that was so familiar to Jews of his time. In seeking to explain the significance of the death of Jesus to Jews (and Greeks), he turned to a symbol they already understood. Driver suggests that Paul thus misinterpreted the death of Jesus for the early Christian community and gave it a meaning that was not intended. Driver also notes that no single image is capable of carrying all the meaning of the reality of the saving life of Jesus Christ.[52] All images must stand in juxtaposition to create a mosaic of symbols to tell the story of Jesus.

According to Driver, a second moment was provided by Saint Anselm's (1033–1109) focus on the death rather than the life of Jesus. In Anselm's understanding, the sin of humankind offended God, and a way to restore that broken harmony was for Jesus to offer his life for our sins. In other words, the death of Christ was meant to satisfy the offended honor of God.[53] Anselm's attempt to explain the death of Christ by a theology of atonement was accepted by church leaders of the time and became part of the teaching of the church.

An additional deviation for Christianity was the marriage between church and state that started during the fourth and fifth centuries. Roman Emperor Constantine, who became a Christian himself, in the Edict of Milan in 313 granted official status to the Christian movement. Major changes followed, and Driver notes that among these changes was the loss of the early Christian community's commitment to follow the nonviolent teachings of Christ.[54]

Both Driver and Weaver suggest meaningful ways of understanding the death of Jesus on the cross. Weaver reminds us that Jesus' death resulted from violence and that his life was taken from him.[55] What would change if we moved from the symbol of the cross to the symbol of the life of Jesus? Then Emmanuel, "God with us," would remind us that Jesus stood with the sick, the captives, and the oppressed, and offered his life—not his death—for their salvation. Resurrection, a new beginning, is the hope we can offer victims of abuse.

René Girard's thesis on *mimetic* violence (from the Greek, meaning "to imitate") is yet another way to understand the death of Jesus. While Girard's reading of the death of Jesus is controversial, his theory of "scapegoating" is discussed and widely accepted in theological circles. Scapegoating is a method by which individuals or groups redirect blame or responsibility from themselves to another person or group. In Girard's words, scapegoating "indicates the innocence of the victim, the injustice of the condemnation and the hatred using the victim as object of it."[56] Killing the scapegoat then solves the problem of wrongdoing and guilt. Girard's examination of "scapegoat" focuses on religious contexts, and he concludes that the method is often used to limit violence and maintain peace.[57]

Girard finds no evidence for a sacrificial interpretation of the crucifixion of Jesus in the gospels. But, he notes, Christian tradition, unfortunately, has interpreted the death of Jesus as the death of a scapegoat (in other words, Jesus has been killed in place of us sinful humans). Weaver agrees with Girard that there is nothing in the gospels to suggest that the death of Jesus was a sacrifice. Instead, the death of Jesus unmasks and calls for the end of religious beliefs or practices based on sacrifice or retributive violence. Throughout, Weaver insists on the nonviolent nature of Jesus and God and denies that the crucifixion of Jesus can be interpreted as a divinely sanctioned or divinely willed sacrifice. Violence originates with humans and not with God.[58]

While some feminist theologians, including Joanne Carlson Brown and Rebecca Parker, have moved away from atonement theology, other feminists have tried to redefine its understanding, and several have attempted to reconstruct the theology of atonement to build new meanings. In studying scripture with groups of women, for example, I have used the text of Luke 14:27—"Whoever does not carry the cross and follow me cannot be my disciple." I suggest that the text may not refer to the cross of Jesus' death, that perhaps Jesus did not know at that point that his death would be on the cross. Although he suspected and even announced his early death, the details would not have been clear. If not the cross of Jesus' death, then what cross could the text refer to? After discussion in the group, the women have usually concluded that the text refers to the cost of following Christ as disciples. They point out that there are crosses that we are not meant to carry, such as the cross of family abuse. They also noted that in any case the call to "take up the cross" is still voluntary—it is up to us to make the decision to become followers of Christ. The cross does not refer to a dysfunctional family, to an abusive husband, or to mistreatment from a parent, situations not willingly chosen by women. The concept of God is crucial to these women: they know that God does not want them to suffer.

Many of these concerns are summed up by Sally B. Purvis:

> When and to the extent that the cross as symbol subverts the protests to and the struggle against human suffering and the violence in our lives, it is incompatible with a Christian feminist understanding of the nature of God and humans. Insofar as those in power appropriate the cross as an instrument of their oppression of others, it remains a dangerous symbol for all groups, including Christian churches, that are still largely patriarchal and supremacist.[59]

Latin American liberation theology understands the experience of the cross as a symbol of God's solidarity with the poor and oppressed. In April 2003 I visited Julia Esquivel in Guatemala City. Julia, a widely known activist and feminist in Latin America, suffered the cruel violence of the war in Guatemala in both her spirit and body, eventually fleeing into exile in Mexico and Switzerland. Her life was threatened for clinging to the truth and struggling for justice for the people, especially those in indigenous communities. She is happy now to be back in Guatemala. During our visit Julia showed us a new meaning of the cross. She said that when she witnessed how the innocent of Guatemala died, she herself was "at the foot of the cross." Those who witness such atrocities committed against the innocent are like the women at the foot of the cross who watched Jesus die. Julia said witnessing such evil gives us the power to speak out, to cry for justice. She added that the resurrection provides evidence for her that love and life are more powerful than evil and suffering.

Marie Fortune, a theologian who is an expert on the subject of abuse, reminds us that the cross must not serve to justify suffering but to transform it. When suffering is present, the cross can represent the possibility of transforming that experience through the hope of resurrection. Like Driver and Weaver, many feminist theologians also shift the emphasis from the cross to the complete life of Jesus, including the resurrection, a message of liberation, wholeness, and justice.[60]

A Theology of Suffering

Christianity has long held that suffering resulted from human disobedience, represented by the fall of Adam and Eve from God's grace. Feminist theologians generally reject this notion and the belief that suffering is redemptive. As Flora A. Keshgegian notes, suffering and oppression result from "political, social, economic, and ideological systems that subjugate certain classes or groups of people." Keshgegian adds that suffering "is manifest through systems of sexism, racism, classism, heterosexism, etc. Abuse is an action of harm toward a less powerful person by a more powerful person. Systems of oppression allow for and encourage abusive actions that cause suffering."[61] Suffering produced by systems of oppression needs to be addressed and the injustice challenged.

To examine the complex issue of suffering, I turn to Dorothee Soelle's classic study, *Suffering*.[62] Just as Jesus was the innocent victim of a violent system, we also experience what Soelle called involuntary suffering. According to the Bible, Job, with his strong sense of justice, was convinced of his innocence and did not give in when questioned by friends who quickly found ways to explain or justify his suffering. Victims of suffering usually have immediate questions: Why does suffering occur? Why me? Why is this happening to *my* family? And then: What have I done to deserve this? Soelle classifies these traditional questions as those "directed inward"; they produce nothing but guilt and do not break the cycle of violence.[63] Such questions often lead people to understand suffering as a test sent by God to make them better people.

A second set of questions is more effective: What are the causes of this suffering? How can these conditions be eliminated? Soelle classifies these as "outward questions." These questions move away from a pure individualistic view to an understanding of suffering as multidimensional, with roots in the physical and social spheres. As Soelle remarks, we need to overcome the temptation to see suffering as natural and to end such a "sadistic" understanding of God.[64]

Once we are able to look at the systemic causes of suffering, we are able to work to stop the cycle of violence and internalize the truth that "God does not desire the suffering of people, not even as a pedagogical device, but desires instead their happiness." Indeed, Soelle maintains that freedom from existing suffering is the Bible's greatest theme.[65] Yet, many women understand their suffering to be ordained by God and to be a necessary part of their Christian journey. Delores S. Williams, an African American theologian, thinks it is important to focus on survival rather than suffering and to move away from the cross to resurrection.[66]

The goal of my work with women is to enable them to see that their suffering from abuse is not ordained by God or sanctioned by the suffering of Jesus on the cross. They must then be empowered to overcome their suffering by finding the power within themselves to turn things around. The "strength of the weak" means to claim one's own power, to use words from the peace movement.[67] These are steps away from impotence or passivity that move forward to embrace the power of life.

Christ is with us, rather than for us, and God is on the side of the sufferer. To "arise" is the theme of liberation present in the story of Jesus, which contains hope for all. The story of Jesus' resurrection is also our story of resurrection and hope for the end of suffering. We are called to learn from suffering in order to come out of it, to question the image of a God who encourages victims to suffer, and to discover a tender God of love who is not patriarchal and will not encourage victims to suffer. We need to gain a hold on the truth and believe that the social conditions that lead to suffering can change.[68]

The story of Christian martyrdom is one of self-sacrifice but a sacrifice that is voluntary and not imposed by someone else. For women living in a patriarchal society, self-sacrifice is expected and imposed from birth. It has rarely been voluntary; in the past few women have had free choice or options. And many Christian women have been taught that self-sacrifice, "even if it hurts, is made divine by the church." It is the obligation of the church to undo these ties and liberate women from the obligation of self-sacrifice. If we have the courage to see the possibilities, change can come about.

Our Anabaptist tradition speaks of three baptisms—by water, by the Holy Spirit, and by blood. The baptism of blood describes the persecution and martyrdom of believers of the sixteenth-century movement. Peter Stucky describes the witness of the martyrs as "an important tool in the tradition of Mennonites—it is all right to be prophetic and to be persecuted."[69] This is the "cost of discipleship" of which Dietrich Bonhoeffer writes—voluntary suffering, a choice. This is totally different from the involuntary suffering that the poor and oppressed experience—or that women experience in their homes. It is important to note that the tradition of martyrdom has been misused in the past to justify suffering and still is today.

Our Understanding of Church: A Radical Ecclesiology

The church is not merely a temple, a building, or a quiet place to seek out. It is a community of believers who choose a way of life that involves communion with others and our mother God the Creator. Most churches of today bear little resemblance to the early Christian communities of followers of the Way who gathered in their homes to reflect on the teachings of Jesus. While women played significant roles in the early house churches, over time churches became increasingly institutionalized and dominated by a male clergy. As the church became more institutionalized, it also became more connected with other institutions, including secular powers, resulting in compromises with political and social structures that occasionally gave short shrift to the teachings of the gospel. Christians today sometimes do the same.

Mennonite theologian Juan Driver advocates a move to a radical ecclesiology, a return to the roots. Our sixteenth-century Anabaptist leaders were radical in the sense that they reclaimed the roots of Christianity, which to them meant Jesus' teachings in the gospels. Driver also maintains (and I see this as a major contribution) that the church is not only to proclaim the kin-dom of God, but that it is *to be* the community of the kin-dom. It anticipates the kin-dom in a modest but real way and offers a sign of hope for what is not-yet.[70] As a radical community of faith, the church must favor life and work against any signs of death; as a body of believers, we must confront the authorities and the powers with a clear vision of divine salvation for the broken world.

The salvific purpose of God is to achieve justice, peace, and freedom for all human beings. While the sovereign purpose of God does not limit itself to the church, at the same time we as the church cannot fall again into the Constantinian temptation to Christianize everything.[71]

The church is called to read the signs of secular events, to discern the authentic word of God, and to work to implement it; the church should not yield to the temptation to try to dominate the world.[72] Just as Jesus came to serve, the church is called to serve. According to Driver, the church should return to the vision of the early church first described in Acts and should reflect the kin-dom of God and its values; it should become an alternative to a corrupt society obsessed with materialistic worries, full of anti-values, violence, and the desire to dominate.[73]

To counteract these influences, the church is to become an alternative community, a safe place for all of God's people. Such a vision helps us live in the world while clinging to a different set of values. It allows proclaiming and witnessing to the world that it is indeed possible not to use violence toward others. The church described in Acts that tried to be faithful to Jesus' teaching bore fruit, shown through the manifestation of the Holy Spirit, and became a new humanity (Eph 2:3–16). As such, the church meets the needs of those who come to it for help. Whether they come with shame, loss, alienation, domination by evil powers, slavery to sin, enmity, rootlessness, or guilt over wrongdoing, we can walk with those who suffer. As an *ecclesial* church, a gathering of the Lord's community, we cannot permit violent behavior among our members, not even in the privacy of their homes.

Peter Stucky describes the church in terms of community:

> The whole emphasis of church as a believing community is demonstrated in the ideal of working together in community, supporting each other in our struggles, interpreting together the word of God, and forming alternative communities. Seeing the will of God for all humanity is all about creating communities of peace and justice.[74]

The church should be in constant renewal in order to be an authentic witness to God's love and justice in changing historical, economic, and social realities. The community of believers should be a new house of freedom where people's hopes for human dignity are present in both faith and service. In the words of Letty M. Russell, we need "a community of Christ, where everyone is welcome,"[75] including women, men, and children, those who are whole and those who are in need of healing. Providing safe places in which to worship and to find comfort means moving to inclusive language and new creative liturgies to heal the wounds of those among us who have experienced suffering and abuse.

Elsa Tamez speaks of an ecclesial community free of violence. "This is the dream of Latin American women," she says, "no more violence,"[76] and, I add, this is also the dream of many women in North America. Tamez notes that "a woman's battered body is the visible mark of the structural sin of a patriarchal society." And if one in three women in the world experiences some form of violence in her lifetime, as studies on gender-based violence show, churches must act as agents of change to end violence against women. This ecclesial community must be one that promotes peace, not one that accepts patriarchal values.[77] Letty Russell has challenged the church to develop a feminist ecclesiology that can help us in "being church." This would be a faith community that advocates for the full humanity of all women together with all men.[78]

IDENTIFYING THE STRENGTH OF OUR THEOLOGY

Three core teachings of the Anabaptist theology of nonviolence can be used as primary tools for making peace that will help us build peace in our communities and in Christian homes: the model of Jesus, true discipleship, and a community rooted in the gospel.

The Model of Jesus

Jesus' teachings focus on bringing peace, expressed in terms of salvation, holiness, healing, and *shalom*. I strongly believe that the root meaning of *shalom* in the Old Testament encompasses holiness, healing, and salvation, understood in a communal rather than an individualistic sense.[79] It is also interesting to note that many of the accounts of Jesus' healing in the New Testament include words indicating that the healings produced multiple effects, not just physical healing or restoration. Jesus' healings appear to promote peace and justice, to be signs of God's love, as shown, for example, in the following biblical texts:

1. The gospel of peace includes teachings about resisting violence through love (Mt 5:9; Lk 1:79; Jn 14:27).

2. To love the other as myself and to risk my life for the other is key to the model provided by Jesus (Jn 15:10–12; Mt 5:44; Lk 10:25–37).

3. Justice must precede peace, including justice in gender roles. Without justice or restitution, harmony cannot be restored in the community or the person against whom offenses were committed (Mt 5:10; 23:23–26; Lk 18:6–8; Mk 9:42–50).

True Discipleship

True discipleship, according to Driver, means that following in "Jesus' footsteps is a privilege and a commitment."[80] Committed followers of Jesus must learn to live a life without violence. This is where the "knowing" must be reflected in the "doing." When a brother or a sister in the church abuses a spouse, we need to persuade that person to return to discipleship. We need to provide an opportunity for everyone to examine his or her life, to change, and to grow. Submitting to the church body for correction is a sign of maturity and recognition, but the church community must be rooted in the gospel and correct in a spirit of love.

Kin-dom of God–Community Rooted in the Gospel

The church should be a community of believers committed to one another in a vision of the reality that will come one day to embrace all believers.[81] We anticipate its arrival by being a place where the values of the kin-dom of God are demonstrated. The community embraces the fruits of the Spirit and love described by Paul in his letters to the churches in Galatia and Corinth (Gal 5:22–24; 1 Cor 13:1–13). We Mennonites and Anabaptists focus on the Sermon of the Mount as our rule of love, and it is here that Jesus clearly presents ways to break cycles of violence toward women, children, and the "other."

SIGNS OF HOPE

In a workshop held in Akron, Pennsylvania, in May 2001, entitled Working Together as a Peace Church Committed to Prevent Family

Violence, an attendee asked permission to share his story. Nathan[82] was an activist in the university when he was younger and still living in his home country in Central America. Raised in a patriarchal society, he demonstrated his manhood aggressively. He married his girlfriend, and even before marriage, he was controlling and violent with her. Later, he had a conversion experience at an evangelical city church, and both he and his wife started to attend it. Nathan began to learn about the teachings in the Bible and he was taught that God gave man the authority to be the head of the household.

In 2001 Nathan confessed that those teachings gave him additional tools and even more inclination to continue abusing his wife. He felt that the church approved. At about the same time, the war in his country began to escalate. He and his family fled to North America, where the family violence continued. His wife left him several times but always returned. Finally, one day she decided never to come back. Nathan lost his family. He said that the church never helped him to confront his violent behavior; it only gave him more reasons to carry on his abuse.

Fortunately, Nathan found a new faith community in his new country. When he arrived at this community of faith, alone and destroyed, the church referred him to a Latino support group for abusive men who, like him, had lost their families because of their abusive behavior. Today he is a leader in that circle, loved by the church and supported by other men who share a similar history. Nathan still cries when he thinks about the loss of his family. The church has accompanied Nathan in his healing process, helping him understand why he lost what he most loved.

When the relationship of a married couple in the church is abusive and the wife is ready to leave, I do not hesitate to support her decision. However, if she decides to stay and her spouse makes a commitment to stop the abuse, we work with them. Many abusive Christian men like Nathan have to suffer the consequences of their actions, and often they lose what they love most, their wives and their children, before they acknowledge their wrongdoing. Many abusive men continue their pattern of abuse in other relationships; few look for help unless they are mandated to do so by the courts. Nathan's story is a living testimony to how a church can help men who suffer from a longstanding problem of violent behavior toward their families. And this is properly a task for our churches and a task in which all churches should engage.

4

Exposing the Roots

In Search of a Healthier Tree

I have chosen the metaphor of a tree to describe family violence because all parts of the tree—leaves, branches, trunk, and roots—are connected and dependent on one another; together they form a living thing, a part of the world's ecosystem. In Chapter 1 our examination of the tree of family violence began with the leaves, those most visible and ugly manifestations of violence that demand our attention. In Chapter 2, after hearing the story of two abused women—Carmen and Jessica—we used social analysis to look at the branches of the tree, those social, cultural, and economic factors that place some segments of the population at greater risk. Chapter 3 turned to Christian teachings in tradition and scripture, showing how they have been interpreted in ways that made them complicit with violence; it also described the nature and potential impact of Mennonite peace theology.

From the beginning my aim has been to take readers slowly to the root system of this evil condition, and that is the focus of this chapter. The power for growth lies within the roots, providing poison or nutrients in an invisible manner. The root system can be the most difficult part of the tree to eliminate. When branches are cut or even portions of the trunk, the roots can continue to live. What is not visible to the eyes of the beholder is powerful enough to keep a tree alive and allow it to regenerate.

CONFESSION OF REALITY

We must recognize that many of the families in our society are not very healthy. Although this is a general statement, it does describe the reality in which we live. Fortunately, many agencies, including those of civil society and government and those run by church bodies and other non-profit organizations, have implemented programs aimed at ending family violence. Even law-enforcement officers receive training in this area as part of their responsibility to maintain peace and order. While all of these agencies and their programs do good work to alleviate suffering and end the trauma of abuse, they often do not provide healing that reaches to the roots of the problem.

Unfortunately, we, including members of committed Christian communities, do not live in an ideal world. The very soil of our world today seems contaminated with violence, a situation caused by us human beings. I believe that patriarchal attitudes, which penetrate so deeply and forcefully into all of culture, are the most significant factor leading to family violence. Patriarchal attitudes provide the roots for violence, which leads to fear, which leads to silence, which in turn is used to conceal violence. A circle of devastation is created from which it is hard to escape. In the words of Mary Ellsberg, a member of the WHO team studying domestic violence and women's health, "Traditional gender norms are a key factor in the prevalence of abuse."[1]

THE NORMALIZATION OF VIOLENCE

Culture is "the totality of socially transmitted behavior patterns, arts, beliefs, institutions, and all other products of human work and thought" or "the patterns, traits, and products considered as the expression of a particular period, class, community, or population."[2] The components of culture lie within the values and behavior of a group of people who belong to a common geographical area or of a generation of people who have migrated to another location, carrying along the traits of their ancestors or relatives.

As has already been noted, some cultures are more permeated with violence than others. While some cultures tolerate violence and others may perpetuate it, gender violence flourishes within a culture of patriarchy. When a given culture is strongly characterized by the presence of violence, it takes many different forms; however, women and children suffer more than men. WHO's working definition of domestic violence includes "any act or omission by a family member (most often a current or former husband or partner), regardless of the physical location where the act takes place, which negatively affects the well being, physical or psychological integrity, freedom, or right to full development of a woman."[3]

The widely known African American feminist bell hooks points out in a frank manner how the culture of violence affects women of color in this country. She uses the phrase "white supremacist capitalist patriarchy" to describe the interlocking systems of domination that define our reality: racism, materialism, individualism, and sexism. All of these are parts of the root system.

Few evidences of the violence present in U.S. culture are more striking than the number of shootings in our schools. Writer Samara L. Firebaugh notes that several school massacres have occurred since 1996. She points out that although it is easy to blame bad parenting and the availability of firearms for these events, they are a clear manifestation of the increasing culture of violence in which we live. She also notes that such events seem to be created by a nationwide addiction to visual acts of violence, and she criticizes the entertainment industry for its irresponsible abuse of its influence and power:

> There is no question that the entertainment industry is an incredibly powerful force in our society. So yes, we need to have better control over access to arms, and yes, we need to work towards a culture of inclusion, and yes, parents need to be more vigilant. But we also need to realize that the roots of violence and cultural degradation are within all of us, and so is the solution.[4]

An editorial printed in *The Daily Tarheel*, the student newspaper of the University of North Carolina, offers a profound reflection titled "A Culture of Violence: Gender of School Shooters Leaves Questions."[5] The article deals with how "the definition of masculinity in America is largely based on physical strength and social assertiveness." The article draws attention to the fact that most of these shooters have been male. It notes, "While maleness is genetic, the American definition of masculinity is socially constructed." Masculinity and femininity are constructed based on the sex of a person and cultural beliefs.

The article continues: "We must also see that we impress certain characteristics, including aggressiveness and violence as a solution to problems, upon boys while we do not do the same for girls. . . . Particularly we need to eliminate violence and physical control over others as part of what it means to be male." The critical thinking of these students leaves us with an important question: What will it take to have safer schools and safer communities? In the end, intervention programs are not sufficient; safety must begin with prevention programs.

WHAT KEEPS THE SILENCE?

In dealing with the roots of family violence we need to recognize the internalized messages we receive as children (or give to our children), thus keeping the cycle of violence alive. We can easily blame our mothers or fathers for these messages, but today we understand that the causes are deeper than that. The conspiracy of "closed doors" serves a function in keeping the innocent ones trapped in the web of this vicious cycle.

Let us step into the world of Phoebe, an abused woman who shared her story. Phoebe described her upbringing in the 1950s in a household where the father worked outside the home and the mother was a full-time housewife and mother. In this house the mother was completely responsible, and if anything happened when the father was absent, the mother would take care of it. "Don't tell your father. We'll handle it." The message was often "peace at home at any price."

When Phoebe was seven, her mother became very ill with tuberculosis and was hospitalized for a year. In the meantime, since Phoebe's grandmother was not able to take care of her and her youngest brother, her father took them to a neighbor's house. While this family looked very normal from the outside, Phoebe soon discovered that it was dysfunctional.

In addition to the cruel behavior Phoebe witnessed from the father of the house toward his own two children, he sexually abused her. Although she badly wanted to be taken away to an aunt's house, she was too afraid to ask or to tell anyone what was happening. After all, the man had threatened to kill her brother if she ever said anything to anyone. Two important pressures directed her to keep the secret: the threat against her brother, and her mother's earlier caution about telling her father anything.

After a year her mother was discharged and the children returned home, but Phoebe never shared her secret with anyone. During her high school years she became increasingly withdrawn, didn't date, and gained weight, undoubtedly aftereffects of the trauma. Then one day at school she heard a fellow student, an African American, react to a comment someone had made about a woman who had been raped. He said, "I would kill someone that did that." Those words were liberating for Phoebe; this was the first time she had heard someone who was willing to do something about abuse committed against a woman, someone willing to stop it. Phoebe recalls that she "fell in love" with those words.

Today, as an adult, Phoebe talks about having survived several abusive relationships to become a loving mother of two children who are now adults. She reminds us of the importance of "looking into the eyes of children to look for what is there but not spoken, because the eyes reflect the secrets that are kept inside." Her long journey, aided by the power of prayer, has ended in healing sustained by one truth: "I know God loves me."

The conspiracy of silence and secrecy that children are taught is damaging in many dimensions, and it contributes to keeping the roots of violence alive. We can argue that Phoebe's story happened in the middle of the last century, but we all know that those attitudes are present in families today. While we can note, as have many feminists, that women are generally socialized to feel responsible for the lives of others and to keep their families together "at all costs," a common thread in the stories of survivors is the web of silence in which they were caught. Only when they share their stories openly can their journey of healing begin.

FAMILY VIOLENCE: A TRAUMATIC EXPERIENCE

For those who deal with case after case of victims of family violence, it is easy to see and hear how the victims have been traumatized by living with violence on a daily basis. Women who are survivors of sexual abuse, child abuse, or incest often bear these psychological imprints or scars, known as post-traumatic stress disorders (PTSD), for the rest of their lives. PTSD is twice as common in women as it is in men.

It is normal to undergo a wide range of feelings and emotions after a traumatic event—fear and anxiety, a lack of focus, sadness, changes in sleeping or eating patterns, nightmares, bouts of crying. If these feelings persist for more than a month, treatment is needed. Such treatment may involve a combined approach including medications and behavior therapy to help control anxiety and to regain self-esteem and self-control.

A report published by Walking Together, a program in Lancaster County, Pennsylvania, makes a connection between emotional abuse and PTSD:

> Victims sometimes suffer years of emotional abuse during which no physical or sexual violence occurs. When the partner feels his means of abuse is no longer effective, he (or she) often turns to physical or sexual abuse to re-enforce control. Too often, sufferers do not recognize themselves as victims of violence because they have not been beaten or raped. Yet long-term emotional abuse often leads to substance abuse, low self-esteem, feelings of powerlessness, isolation, anxiety, depression and post-traumatic stress disorder. A number of studies have explored the relationship between PTSD and domestic violence, finding that 45–55% of women in abusive relationships meet diagnostic criteria for PTSD. Although PTSD is generally correlated with more severe violence, women suffering psychological abuse only score in the significant range for PTSD.[6]

Other reports emphasize that if the symptoms of PTSD are not addressed in a professional manner, "what is not transformed is transferred," which results in continuing the cycle of violence rather than ending it.

EXPOSING THE ROOTS OF VIOLENCE: A BIBLICAL REINTERPRETATION

Two familiar biblical texts use the language of violence. In Chapter 3 we examined some interpretations of Matthew 5:38–39, and similar scrutiny should be given to Mark 9:42–50:

> "If any of you put a stumbling block before one of these little ones who believe in me, it would be better for you if a great

millstone were hung around your neck and you were thrown into the sea. If your hand causes you to stumble, cut it off; it is better for you to enter life maimed than to have two hands and to go to hell, to the unquenchable fire. And if your foot causes you to stumble, cut it off; it is better for you to enter life lame than to have two feet and to be thrown into hell. And if your eye causes you to stumble, tear it out; it is better for you to enter the kingdom of God with one eye than to have two eyes and to be thrown into hell, where the worm never dies, and the fire is never quenched.

"For everyone will be salted with fire. Salt is good; but if salt has lost its saltiness, how can you season it? Have salt in yourselves, and be at peace one with another."

The New Revised Standard Version titles this section of Mark "Temptations of Sin." Can this text provide any guidance in working with abusers and their victims? Is it possible that this text, which seems to deal with mutilation, can be read as healing or liberating? How can violent images and language be used to show us the way to healing and reconciliation? Feminist scripture scholar Joanna Dewey points out that this narration is part of a section that shows that the twelve disciples fail to understand what Jesus is telling them. This section addresses power, and the disciples are warned against misusing their power. They are not to cause harm in any way to the "little ones," who include not only children but all those without power, such as women and the socially marginalized.[7]

In *A Materialist Reading of the Gospel of Mark*, Fernando Belo claims we can understand this narrative in a particular social perspective: a struggle between those who have power and privilege and those without a voice. Belo treats the naming of the hands, eyes, and feet as symbols of the body that refer to Christians who have given in to temptation or yielded to persecution. The consequences of their actions bring down on them a judgment of death rather than of life. The choice is between "Gehenna, a place of uncleanness and death," and the kin-dom of God, "a place of blessing, fruitfulness, and life."[8] Only by following the teachings of Jesus can a person's hands be restored and people be given the power to walk and to see.

Belo indicates that the phrase being "salted with fire" refers to persecution; enduring persecution faithfully can purify both practices and hearts. He notes that salt can also refer to covenant as well as to ecclesial unity and the ecclesial practices of shared meals as signs of peace and blessing.[9]

Joanna Dewey understands the text to address the use of power, giving a severe warning to the disciples: it is better to drown than to harm one of the "little ones." She observes that the reference to cutting off hands and feet that cause one to stumble is not to be taken literally but is an exaggeration in order to emphasize the point.[10] Is such a hard linguistic device truly essential? Perhaps the answer is yes, because this is basically an androcentric narrative. In addition, the issue is serious enough to merit such strong language.

In a well-known commentary on Mark, *"Say to This Mountain": Mark's Story of Discipleship*, Ched Myers and his colleagues see similarities to other "catechetical traditions" in the New Testament that deal with questions of the use of power in community life. The writers of this socially oriented commentary recognize that the call to amputate hand, foot, and eye are "strange and troubling," and suggest that perhaps Mark is using the image of the community as a "body" in the way it was used by Paul. Amputations then can become a means of healing, such as a life-giving surgery for cancer or the painful withdrawal suffered by a drug addict that begins the healing process. In the end Myers and his colleagues agree that the greatest individual and social addiction today is the will to dominate the weak and most vulnerable.[11]

A FEMINIST ANABAPTIST READING OF THE TEXT

Traditionally, Anabaptists saw the sins of humankind as separating them from God. Once a sinner asked for forgiveness from God, the community had the power to accept the sinner into the fellowship of believers. This naive sense of forgiveness has become a stumbling block for women who seek justice and restoration. Mennonite psychotherapist Carolyn Holderread Heggen notes the faulty association between "forgiveness and forgetting" that churches often impose on victims, rushing them into forgiving and expecting them to forget the injurious event. She points out the importance for the abuser to be able to undertake some form of restitution toward the victim, if this is what the victim feels is needed for the healing process.[12]

As a pacifist, I am shocked by the images in this passage of cut hands, gouged-out eyes, and mutilated feet. As a feminist, I need to determine if there are insiders and outsiders and what kind of power is being portrayed. As a woman who accompanied female victims of abuse, I feel great anger every time I hear of a case of abuse of any kind. Indeed, a part of me wants to castrate those men who rape the "little ones." My human nature wants to cut them off from the church.[13] Another part of me wants to use the power of the community of faith to search for more humane, dignifying, and nonviolent ways to manage this painful reality. I must wrestle with trying to understand both the language and the meaning of these verses. The text seems to emerge from a culture of violence, in which the tendency is to respond to violence with violence.

As a feminist, I see many signs in the text of the use of power, the ability to affect the behavior of another group or individual. There is also the power of the "little one" to speak up, to name what is wrong, but, unfortunately, their power is often overcome by the sense of superiority of those with power. Because one of the darkest sides of power is exhibited in violence toward women and children, our goal as feminists must be to deconstruct power relationships in order to transform social values.[14] In analyzing a later text in Mark (10:28–31), Joanna Dewey notes that Jesus instructs the disciples and Mark's female and male audience about what she terms "the egalitarian social structure of the realm of God."[15]

Two of the women authors of the commentary *Say to This Mountain*, Marie Dennis and Cynthia Moe-Lobeda, understand that the "little ones" have been victimized by patterns of hierarchy and exclusion. They understand Jesus as admonishing the disciples that "it is better to be deformed than to conform" to the oppressive culture that surrounds them. In other words, "in a world of violence and inequality," our choices are radical: we either embrace the fire of recovery or live in the hell of addiction. Salt, then, becomes the medicine that will heal the wound (v. 49), and healing can include "reconciliation within the community of faith" (v. 50).[16]

If these readings of the text have value, why hasn't the text spoken to church leaders and members about abuse? The issue of leaders in the community of faith abusing their power is not new. Many cases surface each year, including the scandals of church leaders and clergy sexually abusing children. No longer can we avoid questions of the abuse of power. We *must* deal with them. This text can help us under-stand that it is the desire of Jesus that we accompany abusers in seeking help rather than casting them off as lost. Having said that, I recognize how difficult it has been to hold abusers accountable for their actions.

WHAT CAN CHURCHES LEARN FROM MARK 9:42–50?

In the words of Janice Love, Christians should create models that promote justice in interpersonal relationships within families and within congregations.[17] As part of this commission, the community, out of love, can creatively develop a strategy to deal with offenders—and here our focus is on abusers of women and children. First, the community can help offenders recognize that they, not the victims, should feel shame. They must be accompanied until they come to recognize the destruction that their actions have caused. Doing vio-lence is a choice they have made and also a learned behavior that needs to be unlearned. In keeping with the words of Mark, they need to be willing to put the millstone around their own necks and dive deep into their souls to understand their wrongdoing.

Once offenders have recognized and accepted their responsibility for wrongdoing, they need to work at changing their lifestyle so their hands, feet, or eyes do not inflict harm on others. This process may require separation from loved ones until they demonstrate that they have made the necessary changes that will allow them to return to their family and/or faith community. For some, it may require a total loss of loved ones through permanent separation. They must accept that this is a consequence of their actions.

While faith communities can take upon themselves the obligation to become involved in both the confrontation and the healing of an abuser, they must do so with extreme caution. A need may arise to remove the abuser from the community or family. Each state has child protection laws, implemented by the police, the courts, and social-service agencies, that govern such situations, with the safety of chil-dren always the priority. All must abide by these laws.

Abusers who do not recognize their wrongdoing (in church terms, their sin) can be asked to leave the church body. Even if an offender demonstrates remorse, which is then accepted as repentance, church leaders need to be wary of potential manipulation and must do all that is possible to protect the abused party. (Indeed, church leaders too often confuse remorse and repentance. Remorse is a feeling, while repentance is an action that indicates a change.) Matthew 18:15–17 has been used as a model to solve conflict and sometime restore broken relationships. But used in the context of family violence or domestic violence, the risk for further abuse and the imbalance of power indicate that instead abuser and victim must always be separated to protect the victim. The greatest challenge a counselor often faces is empowering a victim to decide what is best for her and then respecting her decision, even if the counselor does not agree.

A third stage in the healing process is for the church, which is the body of Christ, to learn to love the abuser and to become "salt" to help this person become a disciple again. The last step is undoubtedly the most difficult: the church body, its members, must learn to live in harmony and trust, in *shalom*, with one another. This is not always possible, and in some cases the relationship with the abuser may have to end. The task of the church is to work for peace and healing, which the presence on earth of Jesus makes possible.

A MODEL FOR INTERVENTION AND PREVENTION

As a practical theologian and an educator with the goal of bringing about change, I designed a curriculum aimed at a transformational experience that would engage all the senses of participants.[18] The goal of the curriculum, which I called Learning to Be Families of Peace, is to reinforce the biblical principles of peace and justice by accompanying families in practicing communication and mediation skills. Some of these families had already experienced violence and others were suffering from it at the time. The focus was on the Christian principles of *shalom*-nonviolence, a practical theology embodied in the life and teachings of Jesus.

The general objective of the curriculum was for these families who had been immersed in a generally patriarchal culture to learn to value peace and to deal with conflicts within the family without using violence. Designed as a twelve-week program requiring a commitment to attend all sessions, its four specific objectives were that participants would (1) learn and practice conflict resolution and listening skills; (2) identify the roots of family violence and diminish the events of mistreatment and abuse in the home; (3) begin to study together, as a family, the teachings of Jesus on nonviolence as a lifestyle;

and (4) learn new peacemaking and parenting models that do not rely on emotional or corporal punishment. The approach makes use of both pedagogy and theology, particularly the Mennonite teachings on nonviolence, to overcome the cycle of violence.

The first two sessions were based on "the violence within," a thesis developed by James Newton Poling,[19] to help adults recognize their potential to choose violent behavior in interacting with their loved ones and also to discover the resiliency of hope. Together we searched for God's divine nature inside each of us. Following the principles of transformation of Paulo Freire,[20] each family named the changes it wanted to bring about. Change had to be initiated *by the participants*, so I was careful to allow them to be subjects who would determine their own goals rather than objects—people to be taught by me. As facilitators, we began by explaining that it is not God's will that people suffer and that if they were willing to change, together we could count on God's strength to bring about healing. We sought the following transformations: (1) wives and children who submitted to violence would begin to question the violence; (2) wives and children would search for ways to stop the violence and regain their voices; and (3) husbands and fathers carrying out violent acts would acknowledge what they had done and as a consequence of their behavior pledge to be accountable to the church. The curriculum, on a small scale, implements Freire's "pedagogy of the oppressed."

Learning to Be Families of Peace was taught on twelve consecutive Wednesdays in a small inner-city community church in Armenia, Colombia. The church regularly encouraged members to meet in their homes on Wednesday evenings, so we followed that practice, hoping that smaller gatherings in homes would strengthen the members' motivation to learn to live together peacefully. The initial group included ten families. However, because of the overwhelming response from church families who wanted to take the workshop, we added an additional family. Half of the families were recommended by the pastor and other church leaders. The other half asked to attend the classes after the program was announced at a Sunday worship service.

The Families

The initial eleven families included seven families with a father and mother, and four families headed by single mothers. There were twenty-five children, ranging in age from four to twenty; two of the oldest children decided to stay with the parents in the adult section. Over the three months of weekly sessions, one family stopped attending due to the illness and eventual death of the husband's father; however, the seventeen-year-old son attended every session. The other ten families completed all twelve weeks, with the whole family attending 85 percent of the time.

Of the ten families, four adults had been committed Christians for at least fifteen years. All of the adults had been baptized in other evangelical churches and had been attending the Mennonite church for three to four years. Five families were new Christians with two to three years in the church. One single mother and her three daughters had regularly attended the church during the previous year. As regular churchgoers, the group was reasonably familiar with the Bible, which helped us in working for a deeper understanding of biblical texts.

There was a history of family violence in the six families that the church leaders had recommended for the workshops. Manifestations of this violence included domestic violence (violence between the couple); some degree of child abuse by the parent (emotional, verbal, and/or physical); and abuse among the siblings. Later, when I conducted the initial interview, the families confirmed the violence.

After walking closely with these eleven families, I concluded that the families themselves could not be completely blamed for the violence present in their culture. As María Cristina Palacios Valencia remarks, "In the urge of seeking who is guilty in this social crisis, the family has been accused unfairly. But other factors point to the patriarchal culture that manipulated families into becoming centers of hierarchical power, discrimination, domination and oppression."[21] These are the actual roots of family violence today.

Getting Started

Two weeks before the workshop started, I visited each family in its home. The goal of this first interview, which lasted an hour, was to gather basic data about the family structure and the level of violence that might be present and to explain in greater detail the objectives of the workshop. It was surprising to see the openness with which families expressed their problems. They offered details of past events involving violence, and 75 percent admitted to having used violence in their homes. Family members seemed committed to working for change. I was also attentive to the dynamics of parenting and to how children interacted with their parents and described their family life. It was also important to establish relationships of trust with both parents and children. At the end of this visit the family was asked to make a commitment to complete the program.

Two additional follow-up visits were planned during the three months to identify specific issues each family wanted to address and also to provide feedback to the family on observations made during the weekly workshops. The family visits also served as an opportunity for the couple or single parent to share frustrations and "unload" old issues that had never been discussed. In the end, many of these visits addressed current crises faced by the families. Many crises were financial, which clearly demonstrated to what extent the stress of unemployment was a risk factor. While it would have been easy to blame unemployment for the abuse, it was usually clear that unemployment simply aggravated an ongoing problem instead of being the root of the problem. Whenever possible, we aided family members by providing emotional support through telephone calls and visits. At times of financial stress, we advised families on establishing and maintaining a family budget, and our psychologist was also available for private sessions.

Unfortunately, because of other work commitments and demands, it was not possible to make three visits to all of the families. While all families had an initial and a final visit, only those families struggling with a high level of violence received more intensive accompaniment. It was also difficult to schedule second visits because eight families lived in different parts of the city of Armenia and two families were from two nearby towns, a thirty-minute bus ride away. Fortunately, it was easy to maintain contact with all the families once the sessions ended because they faithfully attended our church. Once the program was over, the families still felt comfortable about calling on us for help if a family crisis occurred.

The Sessions

Each session began with fifteen minutes of worship, including singing, prayer, and scripture reading. In addition to the leaders, each group consisted of members of the families, both adults and children. The five leaders included a psychologist (a member of the church) and a family educator/theologian (myself) who worked together with the adults; a high-school teacher who worked with youth; a community educator who spent time with children aged ten to twelve; and an elementary teacher who worked with the younger children, those who were four to nine. The team leaders met twice in advance to work through the curriculum, assign groups and leaders, and understand our objectives as leaders and educators. A teaching plan was prepared in advance for each session, with the adults and children sharing the same theme and scripture reading. For example, in the parenting sessions adults were asked to evaluate their methods of disciplining their children, and children worked on proposals for their parents about discipline. Age-appropriate approaches and activities were selected for each group.

During each family's initial interview, as preparation for the sessions, we asked each couple or single mother to listen to several definitions of *family* to broaden their understanding of what a family actually is. The term *family* is used in many ways, and its definition has also been influenced and even manipulated by political, religious, and cultural elements.[22] While the "traditional" family has been established within a hierarchical structure, usually with specific gender-based roles, we felt it was important to clarify and redefine the concept of family to include single mothers with children, fathers or older siblings as heads of households, and children living with grandparents.

At that time each adult was asked to draw a picture of his or her family. Simultaneously, the leaders working with youth and children asked them to draw pictures of their families. Then children and parents or adults came together to compare their drawings and to talk about why they wanted to be a happier family. Throughout the actual sessions, an overriding goal was to increase the level of communication among family members. Children and parents were encouraged to hug one another, to motivate positive thinking, to find new ways to demonstrate affection for each other, and to write each other notes of love, which were posted on a decorated bulletin board. Several sessions set aside time for family members to write to one another. During the close of each session, each family reunited, sitting together and sharing what its members had learned that evening.

Program Goals Based on Mennonite Peace Theology

The Mennonite theology of nonviolence formed the foundation of our program. We focused on the image of Christ, the maker of peace, to overcome violence and on the development of peacemaking skills in a family context. As educators, we knew that understanding the meaning of a theology of nonviolence is quite different from knowing how to act nonviolently or actually acting nonviolently. We assigned paramount importance to determining how biblical and theological principles could be used as tools within the dynamics of families to overcome violence and to establish mutuality and equality in the relationships between males and females. We turned to the biblical teachings on peace, Jesus' model for making peace, the meaning of true discipleship, and the nature of the kin-dom of God in which all of God's creation is treated equally with dignity and mutuality.

We listed changes we wanted for the families:

1. Stop violent behavior: (a) learn to recognize it, and (b) learn to relate to one another nonviolently, with no hitting, no yelling, and no insults. (We used a video on domestic violence, *Broken Promises*, to help family members understand the roots and the nature of violence.)[23]
2. Gain better communication skills; learn to use "I" messages to express feelings without verbally attacking other family members.
3. Spend more time together; talk to each other regularly, listening carefully and responding actively rather than reactively.
4. Understand the source of family patterns and thus achieve a win-win attitude in the decision-making process.
5. End the abuse of parental authority; promote better relationships between parents and children, as well as among siblings.
6. Enable Mennonite families to become deeply committed to what it means to be peacemakers and to end tolerance of violence among members of the church.

The Final Interviews and Evaluation

The final interview was designed to evaluate improvement in communication within the family and to learn if the family's commitment to nonviolence had actually brought about change. Generally parents observed a decrease in fighting among siblings and fewer incidents in which they needed to intervene. Mothers observed that their children used forgiveness and "cooling off" skills more frequently than before; there was less striking out at each other, and parents felt they could more effectively manage sibling fights. While most family situations had improved, the parents wanted violent behavior to stop altogether. One family commented that although the change had not been sudden, there had been improvement little by little in the ways family members treated one another, with less yelling, more discussion, and more seeking permission before borrowing.

Adults reported improving their parenting skills. One couple reported that they learned to give positive attention to their four-year-old son, who formerly manipulated them by crying to gain attention. A mother commented that her pre-teenage son had begun "opening up" about his feelings. A single mother shared that she had learned the importance of trusting her daughter. Members of the other families made similar comments on specific parenting skills they had gained through the sessions.

Husbands and wives also reported improvement in their communication skills; they began taking more initiative in speaking up and listening to each other. One husband said he became aware for the first time of how his lack of communication hurt his wife. His wife said that since he began to be more open, he was less explosive when frustrated. Other couples spoke of learning to dialogue and to respect each other's opinion, of learning to be less defensive and to listen carefully. Families that experienced serious violence verbally agreed to a "contract of nonviolence" and to holding the abusive spouse accountable. It goes without saying, of course, that the program did not solve all of the problems of the families; however, the leadership team felt that solid progress was made toward reducing violence and establishing peace within each of the families. Many participants said they wanted to attend more workshops in order to continue learning and improving their communication skills.

Seventy-five percent of the families expressed appreciation for the opportunity to participate in this program and enthusiasm that the program had involved the entire family. The church held youth meetings during the week and women's meetings once a month, but this highlighted the family as a unit. At the end of the program the families classified improvement in their family life over the three months

of the workshops. Families who in the beginning had rated themselves as "regular" moved up to "good." These were families that were
aware they needed help in not solving their problems with violence.
Families who rated themselves as experiencing a high degree of violence moved from "difficult" to "regular"; while this was progress, it
was obvious that moving them to "good" would require further intervention. Of the ten families that completed the program, 75 percent
felt it was successful. The other 25 percent felt that they had received
useful tools but needed additional help in applying them.

During the final visit the participants noted that what had made
the biggest impression on them was *Broken Promises*, the video on domestic violence and child abuse, and the following discussion. They
were also impressed by Jesus' teachings of nonviolence. While Bible
study wasn't new for most participants, they gained a new perspective
on the theology of nonviolence.

Family members expressed their appreciation to the leaders of the
sessions and admitted that they did not know that being a family "took
so much work." Prior to the program, they had not known how to be
a family—that families could sing together, learn together, and express their feelings without hurting others—or how to manage anger.
They also learned to recognize the role culture plays in planting a
potential for violence in its members and how the way in which they
had been socialized affected their ways of thinking and acting. One
woman (a battered woman) commented later, in front of her husband,
that she had no idea that violence was learned and that it could also be
unlearned.

The peacemaking and mediation skills taught by Learning to Be
Families of Peace will not solve all the problem of family violence.
However, with such a program the church sends a clear message that
families living in peace are essential in a radical peace church. These
humble initiatives were positive steps toward the construction of a
culture of peace in our church and neighborhoods. We recognize that
our situation was quite unique; that is, we worked with families in
which the abusers were active members of our church and they responded to the accountability toward the church leaders. Several factors were in our favor: their willingness to comply, acknowledgment
that a problem existed, and their willingness to get help. While we did
have other resources to which we could refer the more difficult cases,
all of the families had financial limitations. With only enough income
to live on, paying for professional help was a luxury they could not

afford; unfortunately, this is true of many families experiencing violence in the United States as well. Although pastors and other leaders are always encouraged to refer cases to professionals and to local agencies and shelters that work at assisting domestic violence victims and their families, the most responsible step is often to take time to connect with those agencies in the neighborhood that can provide essential services to the victims and their children.

NONVIOLENT PARENTING

Developing critical parenting skills is crucial in ending family violence. Generally, an authoritarian style describes a parent who is not necessarily in control but rather a parent fearful of losing control.[24] For children to grow up to be independent and increasingly mature persons, parents must be a healthy influence in their lives. This is in no sense a passive approach to parenting, but rather one that demands a very deliberate plan and model. Indeed, it is the greatest and most challenging task of parenthood.

Disciplining techniques in families experiencing regular violence consist mostly in physical actions—slapping, spanking, threatening—to express authority. Most cultures regard these as acceptable disciplines that are rarely questioned. However, this is changing. A 1997 UNICEF report entitled "Women: Progress and Disparity" indicates that "legislation against domestic violence has been enacted in 44 countries around the world; 17 have made marital rape a criminal offence; 27 have passed sexual harassment laws; and just 12 countries have laws against FGM [female genital mutilation]."[25] This indicates that more countries today are taking this social problem seriously. Although many more countries now have laws about the treatment of children, as a rule parents still see and treat their children as property. Particularly in Latin America, the old Spanish belief in *patria potestas*, better known in English as parental authority, is enacted under civil codes. Currently these laws offer equal rights to mothers and fathers; however, the older versions gave exclusive rights to the father.[26] *Patria potestas* still casts a long shadow, leading parents to believe, "This child is mine." Even parents who know it is not right and who do not want to repeat the behavior of their own parents often end up raising their hands and voices. Such behavior is hard to change. This kind of violent behavior is often used simply to demonstrate power, and parents who feel they lack control are the ones who are most likely to shout and hit.

In the area of teaching parenting skills, I relied on the research that Frank Albrecht (also my husband) has done on nonviolent parenting. An educator with graduate-level training focusing on children at risk, he has developed a program for churches that helps adults and children evaluate the parenting approach they learned from their parents. Children are empowered to report back to their parents on how they feel when they are hit or yelled at or called names. Parents were taught specific parenting skills and asked to begin implementing the techniques and to seek more help, if needed. We offered role models in the way we parented our children.

Albrecht has written an article entitled "Don't Use the Rod or You Will Spoil the Child: Following Jesus, Not Solomon," in which he describes being born into a traditional American Christian family and then later questioning the tradition of his Mennonite church:

> As a Mennonite, from a peace-loving, nonviolent people, it seems like we would be much more inclined to look for peaceful alternatives when it comes to disciplining our children instead of resorting to . . . yelling or corporal punishment. If we look for themes in the Bible, it seems like a definite thread that runs through the Bible, culminating in Christ's ministry, is that of living a life of love and nonviolence.

The biblical text most used to justify physical punishment is "Do not withhold discipline from your children; if you beat them with a rod, they will not die. If you beat them with a rod, you will save their soul from Sheol" (Prv 23:13–14). This passage, written in the Solomonic wisdom tradition, has for centuries been a parenting guide for Christians. Corporal punishment for the sake of respect and correction was defended by Catholics, Protestants, and evangelicals alike by the use of Bible verses.

Albrecht asked parents in his classes to look up biblical passages that support the use of "the rod" in Proverbs and also in Deuteronomy, which permits up to forty lashes for "the one who deserves to be flogged" (Dt 25:2–3). He then challenges participants to question this advice: "What really seems to be the final straw . . . is that we should not be following Solomon's child-rearing philosophy, but instead the principles of our loving Lord. The fact is that in his later years Solomon built temples for other gods, including Moloch, who required the sacrifice of live children." He also points out that much of the research today shows that children who are spanked or beaten at home have a greater chance of becoming aggressive, anti-social, and chronically defiant.[27]

His next question is challenging: "How are we as Christians, followers of Jesus Christ, different from our neighbors in the way we raise our children?" He then cites a long list of readings from the New Testament that provide information on building healthy relationships and guidelines on how to raise children peacefully and encourages their study. Some examples are 1 Corinthians 13; Matthew 5:38–48; Galatians 5:16—6:1; Ephesians 4:1–3; 4:25—5:1; 5:21; 6:1–4; Colossians 3:12–14; and 1 John 4:16–21.

One longstanding Christian who attended the parenting workshops asked, "Why are we stuck on the Old Testament way of bringing up our children, if as Christians we are trying to follow Jesus' teachings?" Albrecht responded: "I don't remember ever hearing a sermon on disciplining children that didn't include Solomon's advice on sparing the rod and spoiling the child. It is hard for me to understand why, as Christians in the twenty-first century, we are not following the teachings of Christ who, in Matthew 5:48, encourages us to be perfect and full of love, and of Paul, who encourages us to be 'reformed by the renewing of our minds' (Rom 12:2)."

The intention of discipline is to develop self-control and character. In order to discipline their children, parents must first learn to control their own emotions. The approach Albrecht recommends is based on "disciplining with love and logic," a method developed by Jim Fay and Foster Cline.[28] If parents create an atmosphere that is unpleasant or filled with fear, the emotions experienced may have greater weight than what is actually said. Discipline undertaken because children have made a wrong choice should motivate the child to think about the bad choice he or she has made and not about the anger of the parent. Albrecht advises:

> If we choose to follow Jesus' philosophy on relating to each other peacefully, we will raise our children to be responsible but will do so without instilling unnecessary fear. In so doing, we cannot guarantee that our children will turn out the way we think they should, but we are raising the odds that they might love God and live life to the fullest![29]

Albrecht sets aside one session of his program on parenting skills to talk about anger. He asks parents to recall their negative experiences of parental discipline when they were children and to consider how these experiences might have influenced their own style of parenting. He suggests that they begin to question the teachings carried down from one generation to the next, particularly the use of physical punishment as a legitimate tool for discipline. Parents are also asked to inventory how they are handling their own anger: How do they experience anger? Are they struggling to control their emotions?

Albrecht encourages children to participate in controlling anger. He takes to heart the advice of the apostle Paul concerning Christian households: "Be subject to one another out of reverence for Christ" (Eph 5:21). If he raises his voice, his daughters have the right to prescribe consequences. There have been many days when he has gone twenty-four hours without any kind of sweets because the house rule is that "if people do not act sweet, they need to reflect on that by not eating anything with sugar in it." And his seven-year-old daughter has been known to say: "Yes, Daddy, I forgive you for raising your voice, but you do need a consequence to help you remember your error. Tomorrow needs to be a no-coffee day!" His willingness as a parent to submit to discipline creates a model for the children and teaches the value of mutual respect.

Albrecht's professional training and experience and his many years as an active pacifist in the Mennonite tradition have been enhanced by lots of hands-on experience with his own daughters. He concludes: "I believe strongly that children need to be corrected. Our daughters know what the rules are in our home, and they also know there are consequences for not following them. I am confident, however, that excluding corporal punishment is the way I will go in parenting. I trust that in doing this there will be a higher possibility that they turn out to be responsible adults and handle their own anger in nonviolent ways."[30]

Parenting skills are highly effective in helping families become families of peace instead of families in pieces, but the principles must be practiced daily. Parents must agree on the principle of not producing more violence and of working together to both discipline and protect their children. As Kahlil Gibran reminds us in *The Prophet*, "Our children are not our own." We need to respond to this loan from our Creator, to be accountable for our actions, and to do our part to contribute to peace on earth.

Frank Albrecht has written many poems about family life. Here is an excerpt from one entitled "Rituals That Form Character."[31]

Rituals are habits
That have a spiritual base,
And when carefully thought and planned,
Help our children run their race.

Our families have but only one chance
To walk their journey of life,
And if there are great patterns formed early on
The family avoids great strife.

There are rituals that can be set in place
Across cultures, societies and time.
Some require a bit of money,
And others don't cost a dime. . . .

FAMILY THERAPY AND VIOLENCE

Two leading experts on family therapy, Salvador Minuchin and Michael P. Nichols, have pointed out that when parents mistreat children, "the real anger is often at the other parent—especially when the two are in conflict."[32] And similarly, Nichols notes that it is believed by some that children's misbehavior is a manifestation of conflict between the parents.[33] Minuchin and Nichols as family therapists understand the family as a system, "a product of interaction in which behavior is constructed in the reciprocal give-and-take of interdependent social beings." Thus the change in one person will result in a change in the system.[34] Generally, family therapists accompany family members to help find solutions to crises and to break destructive patterns of behavior that weaken or destroy peaceful family life. The program used in Colombia and here in North America is informed by this model. We focus on what goes on *between* people, the ways families are organized, and the ways in which members communicate. As families understand how their particular family works, they increase their ability to solve problems within the system.

When I was working with a family and communication seemed to break down, using some of the techniques of Michael Nichols, I would occasionally ask a particular person, "What do you want to see change?" An outsider can often be effective in helping members of a family understand more clearly what needs to change and what options might exist, serving as the equivalent of turning on the light in a dark room. When confronted with the evidence of family violence, facilitators test the ability of the family members to name the problem, to search for its roots, and to identify internal solutions. The overall goal is to help family members see for themselves that violent acts are a manifestation of a larger problem and to seek out the roots in order to end the behavior. The roots of much family violence evidently are found in the patriarchal nature of a culture that normalizes violence or in beliefs thought to be those of the church. They can also be rooted in past abuse, brokenness of the soul, feelings of not being valued as a person—and the list goes on. These are areas where changes need to occur and the changes must come from within the family.

Another factor to be aware of is that many families are in transition. These are often composed of people who still carry old models in their hearts while trying to understand new roles with their minds. Jessica and her father, Julian, described in Chapter 2, are members of a family in transition. Julian stayed at home because he could not find a job and his wife worked five days a week cleaning houses. Julian, who came from a very traditional, rural, male-oriented culture, felt unvalued and frustrated in this new role and apparently took out some of his frustration on his daughter, Jessica. Controlling Jessica was a way to express his manhood, since his wife was not at home as much and as the wage-earner was feeling more independent. While Julian took on his domestic role physically, he did not accept it emotionally or mentally.

As families are increasingly in transition, primarily because of social and economic factors, the ways in which husband and wife see each other and their expectations about sharing family responsibilities also change. Are roles becoming more symmetrical and less patriarchal? While there is no ideal structure for a family, as Nichols points out, a healthy family should have both clear boundaries and flexibility. Nichols does adds a third component, "hierarchical organization," with clear signs of authority from the parents to the children.[35]

There is general agreement, especially among feminists, that hierarchy has been problematic where male and female role models are traditional and that hierarchy leads to the abuse of power with women and children as its victims. Hierarchical relationships that go from top to bottom are an intrinsic feature of patriarchy.[36] Replacing a man with a woman is not a solution. Theologian Letty Russell has pointed out in terms of the church that the symbol of an egalitarian structure can be that of a round table. It would seem that this symbol could also be applied to the structure of a family; experience, ability, and preferences would not be based on gender differences. Obviously, clear boundaries would have to be set, particularly between adults and children, but flexibility would also have a function.

A significant criticism of the use of family therapy to end family violence is that generally no single person is held responsible for the violence.[37] Again, feminists agree that those who reproduce the patriarchal structures are most likely responsible. And men who abuse women do need to be held accountable for their actions. Ruth Krall affirms these concerns:

> For feminist theologians and feminist clinicians in the arena of family violence (in all of its various forms), tension exists between the theoretical construct of family systems theory (and practice) in which the entire system is seen as the locus of family pathology and between feminist awareness that this diffuses responsibility for the act of violence itself. It is important to remember that in any form of intimate violence, moral and practical responsibility for any given act of violence lies totally within the perpetrator.[38]

Virginia Satir, another widely known family therapist, emphasizes the importance of hope. She writes: "There is hope that your life can change, because you can always learn new things." She focuses her intervention on raising self-esteem, developing congruent communication, and encouraging people to be fully human in the belief that in these areas family members are most likely to make the necessary changes themselves. Feelings, thoughts, and behavior are learned, and thus can be relearned. For Satir, the goal of therapy is not to focus on the problem but to emphasize the hope—to enter into the process with a positive feeling.[39]

While there are many approaches to bringing about change in families, both Minuchin and Satir are clear that the answers to the problems of families need to come from the family members. The role of facilitators is to "turn on the light" and point out healthy choices that lie within their grasp.

CONFRONTING THE ROOTS OF VIOLENCE

In working with families experiencing violence, the ultimate goal is to stop the violence. While change can come about through providing family members with specific skills—acquiring better parenting techniques, learning to improve communication, to express feelings, to manage anger, and to resolve conflicts—these are but tools. They will not be effective in ending violence if patriarchal values remain at the heart of the family.

Salvador Minuchin observes that transformation occurs when the therapist is no longer present and the family has actually changed and maintained its patterns of behavior over a period of time.[40] New dynamics should emerge among the family members along with the behavioral changes, and families will preserve these healthier patterns through self-maintenance.

A good example of this kind of transformation took place when parents stopped spanking their children. The children gave witness to this. First, parents were challenged in their belief that hitting was right. They were then given alternatives to use instead of yelling or hitting. And once parents put their new skills into practice, new patterns and new relationships developed.[41] In a culture that accepts family violence, parents are convinced that spanking or hitting is the only way to exercise authority and power. Unlearning such a deep conviction goes against the concept of authority they have known since their childhood. But the ability of parents to confess their feelings of guilt when hitting their children out of anger, their fear of hurting them, and their willingness to try something new indicated they were moving in the right direction. In our pastoral work with the families we accompany, we did not only strive to teach them new concepts but also to minister to their internal pain as well. A discerning and prayerful spirit is essential as we talk together about the biblical principles of nonviolence with the goal of changing not only actions but also hearts and minds.

Most of the families we work with admit their struggles and their inability to manage conflict, although they do try to minimize some of their problems. We enter their homes with patience and love as an extension of our church. When the doors open, we promise confidentiality and respect for the uniqueness of each family before we offer the possibility of change. We also agree that our own lives must illustrate how peacefully family members can live together in witness to the peace teaching of Jesus, and that this is also true of each family we work with. After all, our program was developed to overcome family violence by a people of peace who take the teachings of Jesus seriously. It grew from our desire to be a peacemaking church in our private lives but also in the public extension of our lives. Restoring broken relationships among family members (whenever possible) reinforces the peacemaking values of all of our church families.

What does a healthy, peaceful Christian family look like? We adopt a pledge of nonviolence, aimed at enabling the type of family we wish to see in our Christian homes. In order to create peace, we need to start with ourselves, as persons and as families. We need to commit ourselves not to use violence—physical, emotional, verbal, or mental—in our homes and the community that surrounds us. The pledge reads:

> I commit myself not to act violently, and to work toward peace in words and in actions, to respect others and myself, to articulate better communication, to listen carefully, to forgive with the heart, to believe there is no difference in value between women and men, and to be brave in denouncing violence.[42]

TRANSFORMATION AS A GOAL

It is always satisfying to establish an awareness or consciousness of a complex problem such as family violence. But it was clear from the beginning that our goal went beyond raising consciousness; the goal was and is transformation. In *Pedagogy of the Oppressed*, Paulo Freire describes beautifully what transformation is. The pedagogy of the oppressed not only seeks to transform those who are feeling oppressed, but to change their actual situation of oppression. It means to hope and work toward meaningful change. It is a liberation practice done *with* the people, never *for* them. In a transformational pedagogy, the people rescue their sense of being subjects of history, not just objects.[43]

This kind of pedagogy affirms people's suspicion of the truth that it is not God's will that we suffer, but rather someone else's choice to harm us. Transformation begins when the vulnerable members of a family who experience oppression start to question the violence and struggle to stop it, regaining their voices in the process.

SIGNS OF HOPE IN THE MIDST OF DESPAIR

As women and girls usually suffer most from family violence, we felt a need to determine if the quality of women's lives changed in a positive way as a result of changes within their families. Of course, the answer to this question is quite subjective and also dependent on the verbal skills of each woman. The two women in the group who had been victims of family violence for a long time found their voices during the three months. They not only talked about their situation but also cried out, "No more!" In the end, they opted for separation. I supported their decision and continued to visit them regularly. One other woman transformed her position in the family by starting a small business to help support her family. Up to that time she had been too frightened by the verbal and emotional violence of her husband to take any action. The husband, in turn, made a public commitment not to abuse her. While there is no guarantee that his violent behavior has completely ended, at least she has taken control of a substantial part of her life.

The single mothers were particularly grateful for support in parenting. They reported that in the churches they used to attend, they simply went for worship. In our small church, in addition to developing parenting skills, their children had father figures, male leaders who served as healthy male role models. A single mother of three children who had a live-in boyfriend who drank heavily found the courage to end the relationship, deciding it was better to live alone peacefully than to live with a man who did not share her values.

Life is complex, and clear, happy endings are not always possible. However, each woman took away new peacemaking skills that she is putting into practice. These skills are making a difference in their lives; they are walking away from abusive partners, abusive pasts, and abusive ways of parenting. Only time will tell if their choices for change will result in real and long-lasting transformation. In all cases, one of the most important aspects of the program came early on—someone was willing to listen, to hear their stories.

Telling your story to someone willing to listen is a vital step in the healing process. In *Red Thread: A Spiritual Journal of Accompaniment, Trauma, and Healing*, Jennifer Atlee-Loudon shares her experience of trauma while working in Nicaragua as a Witness for Peace in the mid 1980s. The trauma of her emotional wounds caused nightmares, and in the end she found healing by telling others about what she had seen.[44] She wrote "The Cryin' One" as part of her healing process:

> Come close child and listen to me.
> I'm so full of the pain of my people. So, so full
> Of all that's gotta change,
> Of all the things that happened.
> God don't forget
> And we ain't movin' till every tear is wiped dry,
> Every single tear,
> They all count.
> The human race ain't movin'
> Till we heal and learn to live right.[45]

My friend Kim also found healing through telling her story, but hers is quite different. Raised in a Christian home and attending church regularly, she realized that her mother did not live out her Christian principles. She, and her father, both suffered physical, verbal, and emotional abuse at the hands of her mother. When she confided in her father, she was told, "I want her [the mother] to be happy." She says:

> I did not want anything to do with my mother, and I still feel I have to protect myself and my family from her intrusions for as long as I live. Today I am a mother with teenage children and, yes, I can see how my mother's abuse affected the way I have corrected my children and how I relate to my husband. I was ordering my husband around just like my mom did to my dad. My manner of disciplining my children was very similar to my mother's, but at the time, it felt normal to me.
>
> It was not until I was thirteen or fourteen that I realized that there was a different way of living—that it was actually possible to have a positive family atmosphere. I stayed over at friends' houses and saw nurturing parents, mothers and fathers who listened and who helped their children through tough times.
>
> I longed to have what they had. My father was doing the best he could, but he was also abused, and so I put up a wall. Although he wanted to be more nurturing, I did not let him get closer because I thought he was just like my mother. When I was an adult, I realized that he was probably hurting as much as I.

Eventually (when my brother and I were adults and no longer at home), my mother forced my dad out of the house and they divorced. Almost a decade later they remarried and there have been many ups and downs in the marriage. One day she announced that she was leaving him. That early summer day my dad committed suicide. It was his way of saying "I've had enough."

Very few people in the church community were aware of the abuse my father suffered. Most people thought my parents had an ideal marriage because my mother could be very charming; my father never talked much because he didn't want people passing judgment on him or my mother.

Abuse and the suicide of my father have marked my journey of life. I want the church to be aware that abuse exists inside and outside of the church. It should not be taken lightly. Church leaders and members needs to be educated about family violence and how they can support and encourage people in abusive situations. Reading a Bible passage and saying a prayer is not sufficient. This is a problem that cannot be spiritualized; this is not a question of demons to be cast out. People need real help and ongoing support as they move from abuse to healing. They need to learn of the resources available to help both abuser and abused.

My father did not get to experience a journey of healing as I'm doing now. The path he took was not what we wanted for him, but in sharing our story, I'm able to give voice to my father's pain and offer hope to others.

This is what our churches can do: listen, wipe tears, offer skills, and work at transforming family life, each a step toward ending violence. We start with the leaves of the tree, the bruises and tears that we witness, and then we are called to go deeper to the causes of the violence. Pulling up the roots that lead to violence and replacing them with roots of peace based on the teachings of Jesus begins the journey of healing. There is a role for pastors, Christian counselors, and church members in general to contribute positively to the solution, but this means a new way of being church, a new way of interpreting biblical texts, and a new way of witnessing to the value of family. In the midst of a culture of violence, there is a place for peace churches and a role for peacemakers who can begin constructing a culture of peace in our hearts, our minds, our bodies, and our families. The teachings of Jesus about nonviolence show us the way, but the work of building the foundation of a culture of peace is ours to do. Only through our minds, hands, and commitment can God's peace come about "on earth as it is in heaven."

5

Peace That Brings Healing

Constructing a culture of peace in a world of violence is not an easy task, and certainly not one to be taken on lightly. It will require a very strong commitment to transformation and much hard work. It is essential to find the hidden light of peace in the world of today that lives within each of us. We need to abandon violence in all its forms and learn new patterns of behavior that are nonviolent. While this will not be easy or happen overnight, two transforming forces we can always rely on are having a God of peace whose Son witnessed powerfully to the meaning of peace, and our belief in a God whose love, mercy, and wisdom guide our way.

BUILDING A CULTURE OF PEACE

The context of the twenty-first century so far is one of insecurity: the war against terrorism, fear of the unknown, and deep concern about the effects on our world of global warming. Today the United States is engaged in war in Iraq and Afghanistan, with high levels of anxiety about events in Iran and throughout the rest of the Middle East. Violence rages from Myanmar to Darfur to the streets of most cities in this country. There is concern that tomorrow will bring other "enemies" to fear and to fight. Since we live with violence at so many levels of our lives, we seem to have normalized violence; it is accepted in video games, on television, in films, in the lyrics of music plugged directly into people's ears, and in all forms of popular entertainment. But there are still portions of the American population who believe this is not God's will for us and are willing to work for change.

We need an image before us of a world without violence, an image similar to the dream of Martin Luther King, Jr. Dr. King's dream was powerful because, first, it questioned the status quo of racism and discrimination from which African Americans in this nation suffered for more than three centuries. Second, it moved people to believe that change was possible. Although overcoming the monster of segregation and racism seemed nearly impossible, Dr. King and other African American leaders believed in the dream and made many sacrifices to bring an end to white supremacy. While much work remains to be done, as a prophet of his time, Martin Luther King, Jr., had a clear sense of how this dream would look once it was accomplished. Although more than forty years later we are still not there, his dream is yet before us, in spite of continuing obstacles—with some coming from the highest court in the country. The nonviolent teachings of Jesus provide us with a similar image of what is possible. Can we dream of a world without violence? We Christian peacebuilders believe it is possible, as do other Christians and followers of other world religions, but we acknowledge that it will take much hard work.

If violence begins with hate, anger, intolerance, impatience, and unfair judgments, then peace will start with love, respect, tolerance, patience, and acceptance. These latter qualities are the fruits of the Spirit described by Paul in Galatians: "By contrast, the fruit of the Spirit is love, joy, peace, patience, kindness, generosity, faithfulness, gentleness, and self-control" (5:22–23). These are values from the kindom of God that produce nonviolent patterns of behavior.

Perhaps the problem is not a lack of values or an ignorance of them but rather the inconsistency with which we pursue them in our lives. The Catholic bishops of this country summarized this inconsistency in their pastoral message on violence in November 1994, "Our society needs a moral revolution to replace a culture of violence with a renewed ethic of justice, responsibility, and community."[1] This was a call to Catholic communities in the mid-1990s to confront the culture of violence with a commitment to life, a vision of hope, and a call to action.

Before initiating work to construct a culture of peace, we need to agree on the meaning of peace. I prefer a definition based on the concept of health: peace-*shalom* is a state of harmony in which the mind and body enjoy complete physical, mental, and social well-being, both alone and in the company of other human beings. Peace is far more than just the absence of war, sickness, or calamity. As Christians, our major resources are the example and teaching of Jesus Christ the peace-maker and the values of the kin-dom of Christ-Sophia. As I learned in Colombia, there cannot be peace without justice for the poor and oppressed, and particularly for women.

The International Search for Peace

A culture of peace is being embraced by religious organizations and also by the secular world through the United Nations. In 1945 the Constitution of UNESCO proclaimed, "Since wars begin in the minds of men, it is in the minds of men that defenses of peace must be constructed." Although regional wars continued to dominate the last half of the twentieth century, in a series of actions and publications to launch the twenty-first century the United Nations called for a transi-tion from the culture of war to a culture of peace, which it defines as "a set of values, attitudes, traditions and modes of behavior and ways of life" that "reject violence and endeavor to prevent conflicts by tack-ling their root causes to solve problems through dialogue and nego-tiation" among individuals, groups, and nations.[2] For peace and non-violence to prevail, we need to begin by promoting respect for all human rights and ensuring equality between women and men.

In 1919, following World War I, the International Federation of University Women was founded by women graduates who believed in the importance of working together for peace, international under-standing, and friendship. Two of its goals were to promote lifelong education for women and girls and to promote international coopera-tion, friendship, peace, and respect for human rights for all, without regard for gender, age, race, nationality, religion, political opinion, sexual orientation, or other status. Education was emphasized "to ad-vance the status of women and girls," and to "enable women and girls to apply their knowledge and skills in leadership and decision-making in all forms of *public and private life*."[3] The International Federation of University Women realized early on that women have the power to provide a uniquely humanitarian role in fostering a culture of peace and that this power also exists within the family where, ideally, peace and harmony are taught by example. Today we speak of both peace-making and peacebuilding as keys to the development of a peaceful society.

Women and Research on Peacemaking

Until the end of the twentieth century, Western research focused almost entirely on outer peace—peace among groups in conflict—and neglected issues of inner peace or of peace within smaller units such as the family. However, during the 1970s and 1980s, feminist peace researchers included within their analysis of violence the dimension of structural violence.[4] The new definition of peace then included not only ending organized violence, such as war, but also doing away with unorganized violence, such as rape or violence in the home. The concept of structural violence was similarly expanded to include violence that harms or discriminates against particular individuals or groups. This feminist peace model argued for the eradication of all types of violence, moving from the individual to the global level, as essential to a peaceful planet. As women drew together in their struggle against all types of violence, they developed spiritual resources, what they called a spirituality of life, to resist the oppressive and violent influences of various cultures.[5]

At the same time there has been an increasing emphasis on valuing positive approaches and desirable alternatives, in other words, moving toward a better future. Elise Boulding, a Quaker and a significant peace activist since World War II, has done much work on imagining a positive future. She understands the subject of peace to be much bigger than the subject of war but observes that it has been unreported in the media. Elise Boulding spent much of the mid-1990s writing *Cultures of Peace: The Hidden Side of History*, raising up the numbers of people throughout history with a vision of a world without war.[6]

As noted above, we have generally understood peace as the absence of war, but peace is much broader than this. If someone is asked to define peace, he or she will probably provide a rational answer, a cognitive response. But if the same person is asked, "What does peace feel like?" the response will probably include terms such as "being at one with" or "being calm or quiet." Most actual experiences of peace within Western or Eastern cultures are related to a feeling dimension, to what is known as inner peace. Inner peace often illuminates patterns and relationships, among both things and people, that were not previously understood.

Various women's movements around the world work toward this broader peace, including such diverse programs as the Green Belt

Movement established by Wangari Maathai in East Africa, the Chipko Movement to prevent deforestation in India, cooperative programs of microfinance, and ecofeminism, a movement that involves environmental concerns, peacebuilding, and feminist theology. As Ivone Gebara, a Brazilian feminist theologian who is a leader of the ecofeminist movement in Latin America, explains, there is a growing number of women around the world who maintain that peace must be holistic and that human beings must embrace living in harmony with all of the created world.[7] Movements such as ecofeminism provide resources for enriching peace efforts and lead to visions of a world at peace. In other words, true peace must engage both the "outer and inner" senses of peace. Peace is not the absence of conflict, but rather the way the different parts learn to work together and to understand conflict as an opportunity for growth.

If culture is defined as a set of learned or shared patterns of behavior, a culture of peace will be characterized by peaceful behaviors and attitudes. The meaning of a *culture of peace*, however, is contingent upon how peace itself is defined. If peace is understood *politically* (as opposed to holistically) as the absence of war between and within states, then the culture that creates peace is undoubtedly using the instruments of war to do so, which is exactly what we are experiencing today in the world; threats and aggression take center stage and the arts of compromise and negotiation remain in the wings. Thus, we must always be alert to what type of peace is desired.

On the other hand, spiritually based nonviolence, such as that practiced by Mahatma Gandhi and Martin Luther King, Jr., provides a model of how one can turn to spiritual guidance—through meditation or prayer—to gain inner strength and resolve before embarking on action for social change. Nonviolence, based on spiritual principles, can be a way of life; it can also serve as a temporary tactic when expedient. It is nonviolence as a way of life that has the potential to help build peace, starting in our hearts and being manifest in our homes.

HUMAN RIGHTS AND PEACE IN THE FAMILIES

Violence against women is now recognized "as an international human rights issue as well as a significant threat to women's dignity and well-being."[8] This was the conclusion of the well-known "WHO Study on Women's Health and Domestic Violence against Women," presented as a final report in 2005. The report stated that, particularly for women, violence is a serious risk factor for health and also a violation of basic human rights. The report offers fifteen recommendations with respect to health and other needs of women. Its first recommendation is to promote gender equality and women's human rights. The recommendations also include creating awareness and ensuring women's rights with regard to education, self-determination (such as divorce proceedings, birth control, and so on), safety, housing, and employment, among others.[9]

What underlies human rights is "the dignity and worth of the human person." As proclaimed in the Preamble to the United Nations Declaration of Human Rights:

Whereas recognition of the inherent dignity and of the equal and inalienable rights of all members of the human family is the foundation of freedom, justice and peace in the world,

Whereas disregard and contempt for human rights have resulted in barbarous acts which have outraged the conscience of mankind, and the advent of a world in which human beings shall enjoy freedom of speech and belief and freedom from fear and want has been proclaimed as the highest aspiration of the common people,

Whereas it is essential, if man is not to be compelled to have recourse, as a last resort, to rebellion against tyranny and oppression, that human rights should be protected by the rule of law,

Whereas it is essential to promote the development of friendly relations between nations,

Whereas the peoples of the United Nations have in the Charter reaffirmed their faith in fundamental human rights, in the dignity and worth of the human person and in the equal rights of men and women and have determined to promote social progress and better standards of life in larger freedom,

Whereas Member States have pledged themselves to achieve, in co-operation with the United Nations, the promotion of universal respect for and observance of human rights and fundamental freedoms . . . [10]

On December 10, 1948, the member states of the United Nations affirmed its advocacy of these human rights for all persons. In 1979 the Preamble to the Convention on the Elimination of All Forms of Discrimination against Women expressed concerns that "extensive discrimination against women continues to exist." The convention continues:

> Discrimination against women . . . is an obstacle to the participation of women, on equal terms with men, in the political, social, economic and cultural life of their countries, hampers the growth of the prosperity of society and the family and makes more difficult the full development of the potentialities of women in the service of their countries and of humanity.

The convention also notes that in situations of poverty, "women have the least access to food, health, education, training and opportunities for employment and other needs." The articles that follow address specific issues such as sex trafficking (Art. 6), the right to vote and hold office (Art. 7), access to education (Art. 10), equal treatment in the work place (Art. 11), matters relating to marriage and family relations (Art. 16), and the specific needs of rural women (Art. 14).

The Preamble to the Declaration on the Elimination of Violence against Women adopted in 1993 observes:

> Violence against women is a manifestation of historically unequal power relations between men and women, which have led to domination over and discrimination against women by men and to the prevention of the full advancement of women, and that violence against women is one of the crucial social mechanisms by which women are forced into a subordinate position compared with men.

Article 2 defines violence against women to include "battering, sexual abuse of female children in the household, dowry-related violence, marital rape, female genital mutilation, . . . non-spousal violence," and other forms of violence. Articles 4 and 5 list specific actions states should take to provide protection for women.

These rights for women and girls, while institutionalized in some countries, are ignored or illegitimately suppressed by law or custom in others. What these rights offer, given full compliance by all nations, is equality and the elimination of gender discrimination. Because the abuse of women in their own homes violates their right to live a safe life in a world without violence, family violence is more than a social problem; it is a violation of the most basic human right, the right to safety. All governments are obligated to guarantee these basic rights to all women and girls.

Human rights were first addressed by the United Nations in 1948 as a worldwide effort, primarily to assist governments in treating their citizens rightfully after World War II and to protect vulnerable citizens against any repetition of genocide or any abuse at the hands of a national government. Today, human rights are more broadly interpreted. Torture by a political system and the loss of one's human rights within the family are both regarded as violence and both types of victims should benefit from the same right to protection.

According to Roger J. R. Levesque, a social psychologist and lawyer, the modern approach to human rights includes protection against family violence. Levesque points out that issues of family violence have moved from the domestic level to the governmental level and even to the international realm. He describes cultural forces that foster violence, including "traditional beliefs, as well as economic conditions, existing laws, perceptions of individual worth, and prevailing views on what constitutes a moral life as obstacles that inhibit protection from family violence."[11] And perhaps the most significant obstacle is the ongoing acceptance of the notion that these are individual family problems instead of social concerns of the entire community.

Legal systems, according to Levesque, have focused on the manifestations of family violence and not its multiple structural causes. This has led to the characteristically fragmented response of U.S. agencies responding to family violence. Family violence is rooted in culture and its structure, and if we want to be effective in ending it, we must turn our attention toward the structural belief systems embedded in the minds and souls of a country's people. Saying no to violence is simply not adequate; what is also required is the setting of goals for structural changes. This is a better approach to bringing about change.

Just as the Ten Commandments mandated respect for life and dignity for the Hebrew people on their path to becoming the people of God in a communal setting, so must the international community uphold human rights that guarantee fair and equal treatment for all. Both the Ten Commandments and the international statements of human rights provide us with provisions and specific rules to maintain the communal good and to meet human needs. Levesque recalls that human rights serve as "living documents mandated for the betterment of the underprivileged." He notes that when family violence is viewed as a domestic matter, it is regarded as private; it is beyond governmental control and better left to private resolution. Levesque concludes that states have a duty to protect family members from violence within their homes and to prevent such violations and that they are also obligated to respond appropriately when such violations occur.[12]

Other aspects of human rights that are of international concern, according to the United Nations' International Covenant on Economic, Social and Cultural Rights, include the violence suffered by individuals outside a family system, such as the sex trade and slavery of women workers and child labor (Art. 10). There is also concern about the power of cultural and economic forces that affect family life internally and externally.[13] Understanding how various economic, religious, and legal issues inform the nature of family violence will also aid in programs of intervention. In sum, today's broader understanding of human rights offers a uniform mandate to respect the dignity of *all*—including women, children, and vulnerable human beings who are exploited, oppressed, and abused within society or within families.

Dismantling gender-based violence requires letting go of male privileges and power and a recognition of the need for deep mental and social change. The creation of protective laws and governmental agencies is necessary, but the most radical change needs to come from within the people, within their thought processes and the beliefs that shape their attitudes and behavior regarding issues of gender. Educational programs can play a major role in reshaping these values and beliefs, but more central are the spiritual and emotional dimensions that need to be transformed.[14] Spiritual and religious leaders must join with governmental and community leaders in order to avoid "band-aid solutions" that cover over problems of violence without bringing about healing.

WORKING FOR CHANGE

In 1993 educators and scholars Albert J. Reiss, Jr., and Jeffrey A. Roth noted in their book *Understanding and Preventing Violence* that "problem-solving initiatives and research programs in neglected areas can fairly quickly make incremental contributions to the understanding, prevention, and control of violent behavior."[15] In Chapter 4 herein I described a church-based program that offers an alternative to families suffering violence. The program, which is geared more to prevention than intervention, requires a group of skilled professionals—pastors trained in the area of family violence and family therapy—to lead it. It is designed to operate within the context of church life, but it requires trained people, funding, and resources. It is oriented around nonviolence and peace and is being used by diverse church groups. It is one response to the crisis that exists.

In the early 1980s Murray A. Straus, Richard J. Gelles, and Suzanne K. Steinmetz, researchers from the University of New Hampshire who were early investigators of family violence, concluded that the potential for reducing violence in the home lies in altering fundamental values and attitudes.[16] They suggest five steps to bring about such change.

1. *Eliminate the norms that legitimize and glorify violence in society and family.* In church life one form of legitimization comes from a literal interpretation of the Bible. Legitimization happens when we justify violence in the home as God's will and then tolerate and even glorify these injustices. Violence then becomes acceptable within the culture. Even pastors have been known to use violence in their family relationships.

2. *Reduce violence-provoking stresses created by society.* The authors cite unemployment and underemployment as stress factors, along with the lack of basic health care, among the poor in North America. These are aggravating factors that cause violence to increase when joblessness undermines an individual's self-worth and interferes with the ability to cope with daily conflicts within the family. This is especially prevalent among participants in many rural or inner-city congregations. In such situations churches can encourage the artisans and other skilled workers who are members or who attend worship to work together to open small businesses or micro-enterprises sponsored by the church. Additional sources of income, even small, help to reduce stress factors; cooperative efforts also provide built-in support networks.

3. *Integrate families into networks by neighborhood and community, creating support groups.* The Wednesday evening gatherings described in the previous chapter functioned as a small support group for the families involved. Participants grew to understand that time and space as appropriate for sharing their daily pain

and frustration, their laughter, and their struggles. The participating families began to realize they were not the only ones in the church with such problems. As living in both urban and rural areas can lead to feelings of isolation for families who do not have relatives living close by, the church can become a gathering place, a fellowship or *koinonia*, that can enrich the quality of life and create a climate of trust.

4. *Change the sexist character of society and the family.* Again, the model described in the previous chapter is one of shared decision-making, equal sharing of power, and a more equal distribution of household tasks. Such a model challenges the traditional teaching that gives power to the male heads of household, and it tries to move beyond that oppressive image. God's desire is that both women and men be liberated from oppressive structures and ideologies that do not contain kin-dom values.

5. *Overcome the cycle of violence in the family.* The most disturbing data on family violence, according to Straus, Gelles, and Steinmetz, is that "family violence is carried over from one generation to the next." While learned or experienced behavior certainly is an influence, there must be a determination by an individual to recognize violent patterns of behavior and to commit to learning nonviolent ways of co-existing. Again, the program described in the previous chapter attempts to teach parents that physical punishment is not necessary to demonstrate authority and that it is possible to abandon the use of force or aggression and raise children using nonviolent techniques. The use of violence to punish children only perpetuates the cycle of violence in the family. Each family member must understand that "violence can stop with me."

Straus, Gelles, and Steinmetz conclude that no meaningful change will occur unless we change the ways in which we organize our lives, our families, and our society. Learning to Be Families of Peace, which incorporates the five steps described above, among others, is a step toward transforming the minds and hearts of church members in order to build together a culture of peace.

In *Intimate Violence in Families*, Richard J. Gelles points out that, while effective treatment programs are essential, in order to break the cycle of violence we need to prevent it in the first place. Transformation programs must alter fundamental cultural norms and values that contribute to the use of violence in the family.[17] Family members must learn, first, to recognize these patterns; only then are they ready to learn and make use of skills to prevent violence. The entire process is one of accompaniment, of walking beside those who are hurting and learning together how to live and work together nonviolently. As peacebuilders, we Christians are called to provide viable solutions in the name of the theology of nonviolence by which Jesus taught us to live.

DISCOVERING THE RESILIENCY OF EACH FAMILY

It is not surprising that some families are more resilient, more able to bounce back, than others. A section of the training program for pastors helps them understand this fact. I once illustrated the variations in families by using many different kinds of bouncing balls; their size and colors varied, as did their density. As I described variations in resilience to the leaders, I bounced several balls at a time, pointing out that "families are like these balls. They come in all shapes and colors. Some can bounce higher than others, some move more quickly, and some have very little bounce. While they are made of different materials, they all work against gravity, which represents the daily stress factors and common conflicts that affect us all."

I continued to explain that with the power that lies within them, families can also bounce back, recuperate, heal, and learn to solve their conflicts peacefully, but some will move faster than others. In working with families living in a context of violence, we must motivate them to tap into their inner source of resiliency as they work through counseling and parenting classes and choose to live out the gospel of peace and nonviolence. Resilience lies within them, and it is the source of their hope for recovery and healing.

Family life specialist Ben Silliman makes the same point:

American families have always shown remarkable resiliency, or flexible adjustment to natural, economic, and social challenges. Their strengths resemble the elasticity of a spider web, a gull's skillful flow with the wind, the regenerating power of perennial grasses, the cooperation of an ant colony, and the persistence of a stream carving canyon rocks. These are not the strengths of fixed monuments but living organisms. This resilience is not measured by wealth, muscle or efficiency but by creativity, unity, and hope. Cultivating these family strengths is critical to a thriving human community.[18]

SIGNS OF HOPE AMONG CHURCH ORGANIZATIONS

While agencies exist to create laws to protect citizens and other agencies intervene when signs of family violence appear, few agencies are capable of dealing with the root causes of violence. These roots often seem like invisible monsters that are impossible to overcome because they are unknown; if we know what we are dealing with, the task before us becomes clear.

Secular volunteer organizations such as the YWCA, sexual assault and prevention centers, and even women's shelters in our cities or counties provide training in understanding family violence. During the last thirty years the Faith Trust Institute founded by Marie Fortune (formerly the Center for Prevention of Sexual and Domestic Violence) has created many resources for leaders of Christian churches and American Jewish communities in this country. The institute's first guide, written by Marie Fortune, a theologian, ethicist, and ordained minister, provides sensitive and professional materials appropriate for all denominations.[19] Partly as a result of Dr. Fortune's work, today the mainline Protestant churches and the Catholic Church in the United States have developed declarations, statements, and women's organizations to attend to the needs of their members caught up in problems of family violence.

The Catholic bishops' pastoral "Confronting a Culture of Violence: A Catholic Framework for Action" begins with a strong statement acknowledging the presence of violence: "Our families are torn by violence." The bishops state that this reality cannot continue, and they call upon parishes, schools, human services, and family life and youth programs to build communities of greater peace and offer alternatives to violence. The text also addresses the dimension of the culture of violence. The bishops challenge us to examine our own lives and to choose to make a real commitment to family. The document also draws attention to the Catholic Campaign for Children and Families, using the words of Pope Paul VI: "If you want peace, work for justice."[20]

"The culture of death," a famous phase of John Paul II, one of the most admired popes, is often quoted. Although he used this phrase during several visits around the world, in his December 25, 2000, midnight homily the pope spoke specifically of "alarming signs of 'the culture of death' which pose a serious threat for the future." He noted that this sin was reflected in many of the problems that continue "to mar the face of humanity," including violence against women and children, the marginalization of the young and elderly and "endless streams of exiles and refugees." He concluded on a more positive note: "However dense the darkness may appear, our hope for the triumph of the Light which appeared on this Holy Night at Bethlehem is stronger still."[21]

The MCC of Manitoba has developed resources to respond effectively to family violence and sexual abuse. Its "Statement of Philosophy" effectively summarizes the responsibilities of Christians, listing seven statements about family violence that reflect its belief that abuse is a sin against God, the victim, the offender, and the community:

- We believe that we are all capable of love, understanding, repentance, and forgiveness. This is what is necessary for us to become healthy individuals and live in right relationship with each other.
- We believe that the use of control, intimidation, and all forms of violence in relationships is destructive.
- We believe that every person has the right to live in a nonviolent environment and that we as a community have a responsibility to create it.
- We believe the responsibility for violence always lies with the person who chooses violent behaviour and not with the abused person.
- We believe that healing is a process that begins when we acknowledge that violence in families exists and take action as individuals and a community to bring healing to those affected.
- We believe that as Anabaptist Christians we are called to work toward non-violent relationships based on mutuality and respect as modeled by Jesus Christ in the Scriptures.
- We believe that domestic violence is a social problem and as such must be addressed by the institutions of education, religion, law, and government, through a Restorative Justice approach.[22]

Family violence and sexual abuse are realities in Christian homes and churches. Victims, perpetrators, and family members are among those "hurting people" whom Jesus calls us to walk with, learn from, and minister to. Churches must demonstrate in practical ways that Christ offers healing for both victims and perpetrators and provides the possibility of reconciliation. It is imperative that our peace churches, which espouse an ethic of nonviolence, address the violence present in our most intimate relationships. The Manitoba program and other international programs of the MCC thus provide speakers, consultants, and referrals, and promote resources on family violence and abuse. The program's mandate includes providing a protective setting where victims, perpetrators, family members, and others can dialogue together. The mission statement of its Voices for Non-Violence program is accompanied by an old Jewish saying: A person who saves a single life is as one who has saved an entire world.

RETURNING TO THE GUIDING QUESTION

Now we must turn to a most significant question: Can we really overcome family violence by reclaiming the theology of nonviolence of Jesus? Earlier we asked why family violence is present in Christian homes. Intra-family violence in Christian families is clearly a theological contradiction to the theology of nonviolence taught by Jesus. Yet, it is evident that nearly all families in a patriarchal society are influenced by this evil. The main question, then, becomes, How can we as Christians resist? I maintain that we must begin by living by the principles of the theology of shalom, a theology embodied in the life and teachings of Jesus. *Shalom* must become more than just another doctrinal concept.

Some peace churches have gained much visibility and recognition by working for peace on a national or international scale. Yet a portion of those who claim to be activists in the peace movement have also found their mission in emphasizing that peace starts at home. It should not be a matter of either/or, because we need to embrace both fronts, peace at home and peace in the world, in order to apply the theology of nonviolence of Jesus consistently. Families of peace here at home can also use their knowledge, skills, and experience in peacebuilding to work for peace around the world.

An obvious response to the question of why violence is present in Christian families is that most churches reproduce the same hierarchical system that promotes domination, authority, and power as positive values, and some church bodies use the Bible as an instrument of that oppression. If a church (or its members) seeks to protect a male offender's image or reputation or if it neglects to listen to a victim of family violence, it becomes an accomplice to sin. Churches can be accomplices through a lack of involvement—simply doing nothing to protect the victims, who are usually women and children. Ignoring the issue can also produce secondary victims of violence, people who could have intervened but did not because they did not feel it was their responsibility or because they did not want to get involved. The church must remain faithful to the biblical teachings of Jesus about peace and nonviolence. It is the task of all Christians to help the church be faithful in liberating instead of oppressing.

In what distinctive way can peace theology contribute to overcoming family violence? If applied radically and universally, the peace tradition can contribute to alleviating or eradicating all violence among our church families. We have access to nonviolent teaching tools with evidence that if applied properly, they can bring about change. But for this to happen, even in our peace churches, peacemaking cannot be just another theological concept; it must become a way of life modeled after Jesus. Our teachings must have integrity, and they must be based on the principles of justice.

Various Presbyterian, Methodist, Lutheran, Baptist, Pentecostal, and Catholic individuals describe themselves as pacifists. As pacifists, they may go beyond simply laying down their arms; they may work for peace actively and nonviolently. While the Mennonite Church, Mennonite Brethren, Brethren in Christ, and other traditional peace churches state their biblical peace stance in their confessions of faith, the religious peace community, which is large and varied, also includes Buddhist monks, members of the Baha'i faith and Jainism, and certain sectors of the Jewish faith, to note but a few. Genuine pacifists will live out their beliefs in their interpersonal relations at home and also in their neighborhoods, countries, and abroad.

As Ruth E. Krall has pointed out, church members reflect the social reality in which they live: "In many ways personal violence mirrors communal violence."[23] Most church leaders know which of their church families are experiencing violence. They may include peace activists involved in international efforts but with broken homes and neglected children. They may be those women and children sitting in church pews, praying for help each Sunday. They may include active church members who sit on church councils and make vital decisions about the direction of a church. However, they all make present in our sanctuaries the brokenness of this world. If churches do not recognize and name the presence of violence, then they work to normalize it, to let it sit in their midst, without naming it as sin.

The two-kingdom theology is undoubtedly responsible to some degree for the failure of churches to recognize violence as sin. This biblical interpretation maintains that Christians live in this world but do not belong to it; instead, they live according to God's will. Such blind separation, wanting to live apart from the secular world without recognizing that we are a part of that real world, prevents us from acknowledging and taking on "worldly" problems. Active nonviolence in our churches, on the other hand, should help us better sort out issues of power inequality. These issues are not limited to international power or war and peace in the world; they also include the family structure, gender injustice, and the treatment of children as property. It is as essential to examine and name the structures that perpetuate violence as it is to study the manifestations of violence.

The theology of peace must also be used to resist violence in the family. We can start by standing up as true pacifists who no longer tolerate this behavior in Christian homes, who name it, and who work with these families to root it out. Only a church that is conscious of this social and ecclesial problem and hears the call to respond can work to heal this evil that lives within. Learned attitudes must be unlearned and good intentions questioned in terms of their actual benefit to children, youth, adults, and families. The process begins with education; raising awareness is the first step in building a culture of peace. Families should be visited, programs should be marked on the church calendar, and time must be dedicated each year to teaching and preaching about being peaceful families.

HEALTH AND HEALING JOURNEYS

Because violence in the family creates such havoc, we cannot avoid talking about its implications for health, particularly the health of women and children. Family violence has a negative effect on emotional and mental health as well as physical health; soul and body of the victims are both injured. I believe that most feminist therapists, counselors, and psychologists would agree that women require special attention in order to progress toward healing and recovery. Thus several experts in the field of recovery have developed new techniques specifically designed for abused women.

Psychologist Charlotte Kasl's sixteen steps of discovery and empowerment are described in her book *Many Roads, One Journey: Moving Beyond the 12 Steps*. Dr. Kasl borrows from the twelve-step programs for recovery from various addictions and develops a pro-feminist focus to empower women. Instead of the usual "ego-deflation" approach that emphasizes identifying faults and taking blame for weaknesses, Kasl acknowledges that most women she has worked with have very little ego strength. Many women were battered or found themselves in bad relationships, and some were survivors of incest. Her program encourages people with dependency issues to "take charge of their lives and examine [their] beliefs, addictions and dependent behavior in the context of living in a hierarchical, patriarchal culture." She insists that any program of recovery must incorporate criticism of the political and patriarchal system that fosters addiction. Because oppression is often internalized (for example, "I deserved this because of who I am"), Kasl's program encourages victims to "celebrate our personal strengths, have choices, stand up for ourselves, heal our physical bodies, express our love for each other, and see ourselves as part of the entire community, not just the recovery community."[24] This is a program of empowerment that allows women to express themselves freely.

The "WHO Multi-Country Study on Women's Health and Domestic Violence against Women" is very clear in its call to all health providers and community workers to join together in addressing those issues that cause violence toward women:

> The health sector can play a vital role in preventing violence against women, helping to identify abuse early, providing victims with the necessary treatment, and referring women to appropriate care. Health services must be places where women feel safe, are treated with respect, are not stigmatized, and where they can receive quality, informed support. A comprehensive health sector response to the problem is needed, in particular addressing the reluctance of abused women to seek help.[25]

The WHO study deserves the serious attention of anyone concerned with domestic violence. In addition to presenting evidence documenting the widespread violence against women throughout the world, it also provides many short moving accounts from abused women from many different locations, and it makes fifteen specific recommendations for ending such violence.

The WHO study, as is true of most studies dealing with violence against women, concludes that the main issues that cause violence toward women and girls have roots in basic gender inequality. It is important to note, however, that gender inequality also affects oppressed men. While the word *gender* is often feminized to refer only to females, it is inclusive of both male and female. Inequalities usually benefit men, but men can also suffer from gender inequalities. In cultures, for example, in which it is not socially acceptable for men to demonstrate tenderness or sadness with tears, men lose a part of their humanity. Overcoming gender inequalities means claiming all the goodness embedded in humanity, the divine placed within brokenness, and allowing it to flourish. The apostle Paul reminds us:

> His divine power has given us everything needed for life and godliness, through the knowledge of him who called us by his own glory and goodness. Thus he has given us, through these things, his precious and very great promises, so that through them you may escape from the corruption that is in the world . . . and become participants of the divine nature. (2 Pt 1:3–4)

CONSTRUCTING A CULTURE OF PEACE

As Madeleine L'Engle wisely pointed out, "Peace is not always something you 'do'; it is a gift you can give."[26] But in order to give peace to others, we must first have it within ourselves, within our hearts. In *Seeking Peace*, Johann Christoph Arnold, a leader in the Bruderhof peace community, shares his grandfather's threefold definition of peace: "the inner peace of the soul with God; the fulfillment of non-violence through peaceful relationships with others; and the establishment of a just peaceful social order."[27] In the end, as Arnold reminds us, it does not matter how eloquent our definition of peace might be or how we might realize it; it is not about the information we have stored up in

our heads, but it is how we put peace to practice in our daily lives.[28]
This way of living peace has much more meaning than peace as simply the absence of war.

Constructing a culture of peace means raising children who believe
that peace is possible. Albert Einstein once wrote: "We must inocu-
late our children against militarism, by educating them in the spirit of
pacifism. . . . Our schoolbooks glorify war and conceal its horrors.
They indoctrinate children with hatred. I would teach peace rather
than war, love rather than hate."[29] Fundamental to constructing peace
is the need to embrace the power of nonviolence as both the means
and the end of our goal. Our thinking and feeling will then inform our
doing. The final product should be acts of kindness and consideration
toward humanity, nature, and those living creatures with which we
share this world.

Throughout history, prophets and other wise people have told us
of the need for peace. In *A Culture of Peace*, sponsored by the Mennonite World Conference, authors Alan and Eleanor Kreider and Paulus
Widjaja remind us that peace has to be made and that the making can
be painful. "In this world of conflict there is no way to peace, peace
itself is the way."[30] Peace involves justice and a transformation of broken and oppressive relationships. Peace, in gospel terms, is always
conceived as both personal and corporate. An individual who has peace
within can bring this sense of peace to the community. The Kreiders
and Widjaja remind us that peace has worked historically, "recalling
the fall of the Berlin Wall, the end of the Cold War, the breakdown of
apartheid in South Africa, and even the peace process in Ireland."[31]
Peace in these situations did not come about overnight but required
many years of work by peacemakers to create awareness, organize
boycotts, confront oppressive systems, and propose peaceful alternatives. True peacemakers do not arrive in uniforms carrying weapons;
they may achieve a moratorium on warfare, but true peace consists of
more than soldiers who agree to put down their weapons. True peace
is a hard path to walk but a necessary one to choose.

Iranian American psychotherapist Shirin Shokouhi has recently
made an interesting comparison between the American involvement
in Iraq and domestic violence in America. He observes a similarity
between the way a perpetrator's need for "power and control builds
up tension that results in a violent domestic act—and the buildup of
tension and the outburst are repeated over and over—and the nature

of the American military's involvement in Iraq and its neighboring countries." Shokouhi concludes: "As long as America accepts violence as a legitimate means to solve conflicts, this psychological and spiritual pattern will perpetuate violence in our society and in our homes. The urge to strike out at any perceived enemy must be owned and disarmed with peace."[32]

Establishing a culture of peace that lasts will require new ways of talking, new systems of communication, new patterns of behavior, and new organizational structures. Churches, schools, families, and all of society need to articulate and live the values and attitudes necessary for nonviolence and peace to be present among us.

In a series of actions and publications in 2000 to launch the twenty-first century's International Decade for a Culture of Peace and Nonviolence for the Children of the World, the United Nations called for a transition from the culture of war to a culture of peace. This requires:

- instead of enemy images,
  o understanding, tolerance & solidarity
- instead of armaments,
  o disarmament, universal & verifiable
- instead of authoritarian governance,
  o democratic participation
- instead of secrecy and propaganda,
  o the free flow & sharing of information
- instead of violence,
  o dialogue, negotiation, rule of law, active non-violence
- instead of male domination,
  o the equality of women
- instead of education for war,
  o education for peace
- instead of exploitation of the weak and of the environment,
  o economies of peace with equitable, sustainable development.

This may sound like a utopian dream, but all real change starts out as possibility. The energy for transformation comes when we know and feel the need for change; then the doing will follow and the power of a few can become the creating power of many. This is the movement of the spirit of true peace. This is the *shalom*, the peace-harmony that is born in the tranquility of our souls as a result of walking with Christ the peacemaker. While true peace may be born in the midst of conflict, it is not achieved by military force or by imposing the views of a chosen few on a majority. It must come from within, from a thirst, a need for things to be different.

All the member states of the United Nations voted for the Declaration and Programme of Action on a Culture of Peace calling for a Global Movement for a Culture of Peace, and during the International Year for a Culture of Peace over seventy-five million people around the world signed Manifesto 2000, pledging to practice a culture of peace in their family, school, and community. This collective movement toward change began with personal pledges to work for peace and nonviolence.

The desire for peace has been expressed by many famous thinkers throughout history. Confucius (551–479 B.C.E.) wrote, "To put the world right in order, we must first put the nation in order; to put the nation in order, we must first put the family in order; to put the family in order, we must first cultivate our personal life; we must first set our hearts right." And Gandhi saw nonviolence as the path: "There is no hope for the aching world except through the narrow and straight path of nonviolence." While some might say that this talk for peace sounds good, we need to start from some place. The culture of peace must germinate within each of us and move outward until it is born in the entire community.

Churches must also participate in creating a culture of peace by rediscovering their prophetic voices to respond to suffering. As liberation theologians have pointed out in Latin America and around the world, responding to oppression and suffering is no longer a matter of choice. Not to respond to the vulnerable of our society is taking the side of the oppressor. Not to respond is the equivalent of telling victims to tolerate the violence that oppresses them. Not to respond to suffering perpetuates the sin of violence. Injustice should not allow Christians to remain neutral.

It is essential for us in faith communities to define a program of outreach and ministry for families that are caught up in violence. Therapists, educators, and ministers within the church need to learn to walk with the victims and abusers to help them identify the roots of violence. As noted earlier, in order to design such programs, church leaders must examine the theology of the cross and suffering and agree to eliminate any historical or hermeneutical distortions imposed on these doctrines.

In Chapter 2 we encountered Jessica and Carmen, two women living in the city of Armenia in Colombia. Their stories demonstrate practical ways in which the church can accompany victims of violence. Jessica has remained a close friend, and whenever I visit Colombia, we talk about her journey to healing. Although her self-esteem was deeply affected by the violence she experienced, she has completed her training as a nurse's aide. Although Jessica's mother and her siblings are working to change the ways they relate to one another, they still revert to violence at times. Out of her love for her family, Jessica is committed to helping them journey toward healing as well.

Carmen has chosen to continue to live with David. Unfortunately, David continues to behave violently toward her and their sons. Emotionally, Carmen is not well, but she believes she is not capable of living without David. The church has sent her food as a sign of support. David, still struggling with alcoholism, has withdrawn from the church. Their older son, Ramón, decided not to live with the family, and the church helped him find a place to live and is also helping with his education. Ramón attends weekly discipleship sessions and is active in church life. He has developed a network of church people who care for him.

Overall, family violence is an opportunity for the church to get involved and to help the victims find strength through their faith and learn to trust again. It is an opportunity to put into action the ministry of presence. As Melissa Miller, a Mennonite family therapist, reminds us, "Our acting as God-with-skin-on is a tangible symbol of the ever-present God whose steadfast love endures forever."[33] In the end, this is the meaning of peace as the *shalom-well-being* of all, and this was the peace Jesus intended for his followers: "My peace I give to you. I do not give to you as the world gives" (Jn 14:27).

RETURNING TO THE ACTION/REFLECTION SPIRAL

A useful approach in investigating areas of injustice is the action/reflection spiral. It involves asking questions, carefully examining the answers, reflecting on their meaning, and then devising a response. In practice, those involved return to look at the outcome, determine if it has been effective, and modify the approach as needed. This process of questioning, examining, and evaluating—often called see-judge-act—continues until the desired transformation comes about. In this case, can a theology of nonviolence, based on the peace teachings of Jesus in the gospels, truly improve the quality of life in the families we accompany?

I spent a considerable amount of time with a number of families in Armenia, Colombia, and also here in North America, and I have seen each family's quality of life improve to some degree. The message to the families was always clear: You are important to our church, and it hurts us to see you suffer. Questions we must ask within the sequence of seeing, judging, acting include the following: What other efforts do we need to make? What kind of follow-up do we need to design for these families? What changes should we make to the program before we start again with a new group of families? Can other churches implement this curriculum without the same number of human resources (a team of five meeting once each week)? Were we able to overcome family violence?

We concluded that we had reduced violence in three families and that in other families members had learned to resist emerging violent patterns. Preventive tools/skills were offered, and family members were encouraged to own their problem and move toward change. They were empowered, taken care of, and prayed for. They were taught social skills and alternative behaviors based on the nonviolence of Jesus' teaching with love and hope. Do we need to do more? Yes, of course. Churches must continue to reach out to hurting families, and ongoing programs need to undergo continual self-evaluation to determine additional needs and devise new strategies. But one of the priorities must be prevention.

SIGNS OF HOPE

This portrait of the tree of family violence, although dark and seeming to be beyond healing at times, does reflect small beacons of light. Some of these programs have already been noted. Two illustrations of hope though deserve further examination. They are the informal networks of sisterhood that bring women together to resist violence on a small scale, and the hopefulness of the Declaration of the World Council of Churches on the Decade of Overcoming Violence.

Networks of Sisterhood

Many different networks of sisterhood operate around the world. In the United States young women at colleges and universities who join sororities often maintain these close relationships throughout their lives. Many of these ties persist (as they do also with men) and provide support and other benefits as young women enter the job market and the world of work. Some older members of the group also serve as empowering role models.

In some less-developed countries, women still gather around the well to tell stories and solve problems as they fill buckets with water, or they seek advice and support from other women as they gather at the river to do laundry. Women have been empowering one another in this way for centuries, and may this coming together continue forever.

Richly empowering networks of women of color have also come into being, particularly in this new millennium. As women tell their individual stories, they share the common struggles of racism and sexism and poverty, finding solidarity and ways forward together. This is a way to resist the temptation to assimilate into the dominant culture and also to find strength in their own identity. Sisterhood nurtures women's minds, bodies, and spirits.

A support group of Anabaptist women was created in Lancaster, Pennsylvania, within the Lancaster Conference of the Mennonite Church, to work for the ordination of women in the churches that belong to the conference. We named our support group FIN. Like fish, we are working to develop fins that will survive the strong currents that oppose us. And, as I reminded the members recently, in Spanish fin means "the end"—for us, the end of religious oppression and the beginning of life in the Spirit so we can use all our gifts to build the kin-dom of Christ-Sophia. We are not willing to wait for change to take place. Although this particular example is not related to family violence, it has everything to do with gender-based domination, because our church structures and church leaders seem to be saying that women in ministry and men in ministry do not have the same value.

Women around the world have also learned creative ways of resisting violence, including the use or non-use of their bodies. Some victimized women, both young and old and from a variety of social classes, have decided to continue living with their husbands but refuse to sleep with them. While such a decision may seem simple from a North American perspective, in a strong *machista* society, that action borders on a declaration of war. Most women in Latin America are socialized to believe that it is their duty to have intercourse whenever desired by a husband or live-in boyfriend. Cases of marital rape are fairly common, even among women who are church leaders.

Five women I counseled in Colombia withdrew their bodies sexually from their partners because of prolonged abuse. They said no in order to retain some degree of self-dignity. Remarkably, the men seemed to understand that because of their violation of the women they lost the privilege of having access to their bodies. While living in the same house, they maintained the boundaries. These women reported that their bodies were the only weapons they possessed. They found the courage to say no to male domination and further violence. In an article entitled "Nonresistance, Nonviolent Resistance, and Power," J. Lawrence Burkholder writes that nonviolence can take the form of resistance in certain circumstances.[34] Women who deny the use of their bodies are thus practicing a manner of nonviolent resistance.[35]

Unfaithfulness in marriage, criticized but tolerated, is an act of violence and sin; it is also a violation of a covenant established within the church. Workshops and counseling on family abuse cannot avoid talking about the growing spread of HIV/AIDS, which is often an outcome of unfaithfulness. In Latin America the largest numbers of women infected with the HIV virus today are "decent housewives." This is also true in Africa and increasingly in Asia.

In 1994, forty-five women from twenty-four countries came together in San José, Costa Rica, to discuss the many issues facing women and to "transcend the barriers of geography, language, and histories of exploitation to build a genuine solidarity." Sponsored by the Women's Commission of the Ecumenical Association of Third World Theologians, the final statement of the conference noted:

> We recognize that the androcentric conception of humanity both produces and is an outcome of the patriarchal and hierarchical organization of societies which objectifies women and their bodies. The violence (sexual, economic, socio-cultural, and religious) endemic to this system that degrades and victimizes women is generally accepted as the norm. . . .

Resisting violence is a deeply spiritual work interwoven with the struggle for life. We must deconstruct theologies of the spirit that devalue physical life, especially life as symbolized in the bodies, and particularly in the sexuality, of women. Spirit/body dualism must be reconstructed toward a whole-life energy of resisting, renewing, sustaining, healing, and growing. Such a spirituality of and for life is continually being renewed not only through our experiences of work and struggle but also through those of prayer, contemplation, and communion in worship and action. . . .

We recognize that the perpetration of violence against women in and by religions, churches, and theologies is a very significant part of each of these discourses of violence. We see violence against women in religion and churches, and it is theologically and symbolically perpetrated, as a crucial area of further discussion and critique.[36]

The group's Call to Action begins with the striking sentence, "Violence against women thrives on silence" and includes several commitments to make women's voices heard by continuing to share stories and to develop women's theological networks, and to promote campaigns of solidarity to end trafficking and to counter violence against women. The statement ends, "ABOVE ALL, WE CALL FOR AN END TO VIOLENCE AGAINST WOMEN. ¡NO MAS VIOLENCIA CONTRA LAS MUJERES!"[37]

Decade of Overcoming Violence

The Decade of Overcoming Violence, launched as an ecumenical church initiative in 2001 by the World Council of Churches (WCC), focuses on seeking reconciliation and peace in a world pervaded by a culture of violence. Rooted in theological affirmations on issues of violence and peace, the goal of the Decade to Overcome Violence is to bring about communities of peace around the world through theological reflection. Directed by the Faith and Order Team of the WCC, its scripture guide is a text from Ephesians: "For Christ is our peace; in his flesh he has made both groups into one and has broken down the dividing walls of hostility between us. . . . So he came and proclaimed peace to you who were far off and peace to you who were near; for through him both of us have access in one Spirit to the Father" (Eph 2:14–18).

For Christians, the sanctity of life is central, and churches must therefore consider the vocation of peace to be a faith mandate. The WCC recognizes that churches have always been divided and continue to be divided on issues of war and peace. Nevertheless, the increasing complexity of the twenty-first century presents both challenges and new opportunities for the churches to work together for peace. Some of these challenges include the ever-widening gap between the powerful and the powerless and between the rich and the poor, economic globalization, the presence of many civil wars and violent conflicts, terrorism and the war on terrorism, a revived arms race and a renewed drive for military security, the glorification of violence by the media and entertainment industry, and the rise of religious fundamentalism and growing intolerance.

The Decade to Overcome Violence: Churches Seeking Reconciliation and Peace 2001–2010 calls for repentance for complicity in violence and a creative engagement with the world to find alternatives. The papal encyclical *Pacem in terris* and subsequent statements of Pope Paul VI and Pope John Paul II also call upon the church to work to build a culture of peace in a world pervaded by a culture of violence. These documents engage in an analysis of violence and encourage the active pursuit of possibilities for peace with justice.

Rev. Dr. Samuel Kobia, general secretary of the WCC, said in a news release on March 5, 2001, that the Decade of Overcoming Violence "has provided a framework for a growing number of churches around the world to address violence holistically in all its many forms and develop creative ways to overcome violence." In 1998, Dr. Fernando Enns, a German Mennonite on the central committee of the WCC, first proposed "a movement of churches in fellowship to overcome violence. What we are hoping for and dreaming of is that churches will connect to it, and own it. Here's an ecumenical space opening up where we can work on this topic." Rev. Hansulrich Gerber, the coordinator of the Decade of Overcoming Violence, affirmed that vision. There is, he said, "a critical mass of transformative power in the churches and communities to overcome violence, and it's growing. We have energy and momentum." The hope is that as the Decade of Overcoming Violence brings more churches into the movement for peace, they will have "new energy to mobilize and work together instead of separately." The Decade of Overcoming Violence clearly asserts that "the way of Christ, who is our peace" calls us to take action against violence. Many churches have prepared materials and designed programs and workshops to serve the goal of the Decade of Overcoming Violence. In November 2007 the Evangelical Lutheran Church in America sponsored a conference entitled Living Faithfully in a Violent World: Congregations and Community to train church leaders in peacebuilding. Many churches have several publications available that deal directly with violence used against women.

It is encouraging that two large world bodies—the WCC and the United Nations—support and promote peace initiatives. While international and national movements, both religious and secular, are essential to provide broad direction and unify resources, grassroots movements are equally important. To be fully effective, change must take place within our own homes, churches, and communities. While we need systematic structural changes, we also need to walk with those in pain and minister to them so they—and all of us—can be resurrected as families.

SEPARATE BUT EQUAL

Much work needs to be done to overcome gender inequality, which lies at the heart of family violence. Ruth E. Krall observes, "Family has a central place in the education of men and women about desired gender roles. Violence in patriarchal families is a necessary part of the culture's desired behaviors. Religious training about women's inferiority is one of the most potent forms of cultural reinforcement. This reinforces familial and cultural forms and acts of violence against women."[38]

In 1896, in the case of *Plessy v. Ferguson*, the U.S Supreme Court ruled that "separate but equal" was the way in which people of color and whites should be treated in this country. It was applied not only to transportation, but also to the educational system, churches, and commercial operations in the United States. It was not until 1954 that "separate but equal" was challenged and overturned in the case of *Brown v. Board of Education*. Great injustice has resulted from the earlier ruling, and both its presence and its scars are still visible across this country today.

To some degree gender inequality can be compared to the evil of racism, as both share the roots of control and power. Different rules of socialization still apply to raising boys and girls, and many women are valued more if they decide to be stay-at-home moms. Some of the more conservative churches even accuse women who work outside the home of fragmenting family life and use scripture to support their views, much as was done in the 1700s and 1800s to justify slavery and in the 1900s to justify racial discrimination. We continue to use religion to rationalize injustice and violence when it suits us. Beliefs and attitudes such as these support actions of violence, whether within a family or on the international scene. "Separate but equal" accomplishes little in the presence of social rules that discriminate against a particular gender or against the poor or against those of a different skin color.

CHALLENGES AHEAD

The topic of family violence, vital to the well-being of our society, is both a social problem to be resolved and an academic problem to be studied. There is a need to merge scientific learning with efforts at social change to address this harmful social reality. Academics and practitioners must be willing to cooperate and learn from one another in order to progress. Academics cannot forget that real people are at risk and urgently need help, and practitioners should not stumble ahead without theoretical grounding.

A similar dichotomy can exist between caring for the victim of violence and ending the violent behavior. If one is chosen and the other is ignored, healing will not be complete. Churches must be particularly aware of this danger, as it may seem more appropriate at the time—or be easier—to provide assistance for victims without addressing the violent behavior that has victimized them. Churches must be involved in both efforts. In moments of stress, when we see signs of a child being hurt or a woman being beaten, our hearts go out to them, but we hover about, not wanting to get involved with the abuser. The preferential option for the poor and oppressed is a mandate that encompasses a call for justice and action to make things right.

We also must stop to ask what we understand by *family*, and what are we trying to rescue. If we do not ask, we may be struggling to save a traditional ideal or a social construct, insensitive to the reality of today. If "saving the family" means saving the male headship of a family, we may be doing no more than guaranteeing further oppression within the family. Or, if we mean keeping the family together at all costs, we may be pronouncing a death sentence for one of its members. Church leaders need to reflect on the concept of family we have inherited and on what constitutes healthy family life. Two messages should be clear: (1) No one is to be hurt, and (2) There will be no more violence. This is when we start working toward real peace so that homes will be safe places in which to live, sacred places of God's peace.

A REFLECTION

As I lie down under this tree named Family Violence, I can see the enormous extensions of its branches as the leaves dance in the wind. It looks like every other tree. Beyond it extends a tapestry of a huge sky of blue with slowly moving white clouds. From time to time I lose sight of the beautiful background and the shaking leaves capture my attention again, hundreds of leaves moving rapidly above me.

Oh! I must not forget the twisted roots that extend deep beneath my body. These roots nourish this tree of deceit so it can live. And I think of the trunk that supports this tree so it may grow. I rest on this earth floor, studying this tree, and wonder where the other tree is— the tree called the tree of life. What does it look like? Has it been overshadowed by this tree of violence? Can we enjoy its might? Can its knowledge open our sight? And I pray, "Oh, Mother God, undo or cut these violent roots below each of us and nourish the roots of life and peace that lie within." As I finish writing, I determine to plant a healthy tree. I will do my best to work for peace. The rest is of God.

Notes

Introduction

1. Linda Crockett is the author of *The Deepest Wound: How a Journey to El Salvador Led to Mother-Daughter Incest* (Nashville, TN: Author Showcase Preservation Foundation, 2001). She is currently the director of the Walking Together: Support for Survivors of Family Violence program at the Samaritan Counseling Center in Lancaster, Pennsylvania.

2. Crockett, personal communication. See also James Newton Poling, *Render unto God: Economic Vulnerability, Family Violence, and Theology* (St. Louis: Chalice Press, 2002), 42–54.

3. L. Heise, M. Ellsberg, and M. Gottemoeller, *Ending Violence against Women*. Population Reports, Series L, no. 11 (Baltimore: Johns Hopkins University School of Public Health, December 1999). http://www.infoforhealth.org/pr/l11/violence.pdf (accessed November 30, 2007).

4. U.S. Department of Justice, *Family Violence Statistics* (Washington, DC: U.S. Department of Justice, 2005); www.ojp.usdoj.gov/bjs/abstract/fvs.htm (accessed November 30, 2007).

5. Heise, Ellsberg, and Gottemoeller, "Ending Violence against Women."

6. Luz Martínez, "¡Golpes No¡" *Carrusel* (November 22, 2002), 1207.

7. Alba Inés Cano Ballesteros, *¿Cómo prevenir la violencia intrafamiliar?* (Bogotá: Bienestar Familiar, 2001), 2.

8. Monserrat Sabot and Ana Carcedo, "Violencia Intrafamiliar—Ruta Crítica de las Mujeres Afectadas" (Intra-family violence: Critical situations of women affected in Honduras) (Pan-American Health Organization, 1999). I was given this information during a presentation in Honduras in 2003.

9. Sophia Chirongoma, "Women, Poverty, and HIV in Zimbabwe," in *African Women, Religion, and Health: Essays in Honor of Mercy Amba Ewudziwa Oduyoye*, ed. Isabel Apawo Phiri and Sarojini Nadar (Maryknoll, NY: Orbis Books, 2006), 178; see also Elizabeth Amoah, "Violence and Women's Bodies in African Perspective," in *Women Resisting Violence: Spirituality for Life*, ed. Mary John Mananzan et al., 80–86 (Maryknoll, NY: Orbis Books, 1996).

10. Hisako Kinukawa, *Women and Jesus in Mark: A Japanese Feminist Perspective* (Maryknoll, NY: Orbis Books, 2004), viii, 62–63. See also Chung Hyun Kyung, "Your Comfort vs. My Death," in *Women Resisting Violence: Spirituality for Life*, ed. Mary John Mananzan et al., 129–40 (Maryknoll, NY: Orbis Books, 1996); and Choi Hee An, *Korean Women and God: Experiencing God in a Multireligious Colonial Context* (Maryknoll, NY: Orbis Books, 2005).

11. Choi, *Korean Women and God*.

12. Emilie M. Townes, ed., *A Troubling in My Soul: Womanist Perspectives on Evil and Suffering* (Maryknoll, NY: Orbis Books, 1993). See also Marcia Y. Riggs, ed., *Can I Get a Witness?: Prophetic Religious Voices of African American Women, An Anthology* (Maryknoll, NY: Orbis Books, 1997).

13. See especially Ada María Isasi-Díaz, "*Un Poquito de Justicia*: A Little Bit of Justice," in *Mujerista Theology* (Maryknoll, NY: Orbis Books, 1996), 105–27.

14. Anabaptist is the nickname given to Christians of the sixteenth century who were rebaptized as adults.

15. Peace skills can be defined generally as learning how to express feelings in a healthy way, regardless of the stimulus, through active listening, anger management, reading body language, and developing the ability to communicate fluently even under stress.

1. Examining the Leaves

1. R. Jewkes, P. Sen, and C. Gracia-Moreno, "Sexual Violence," in *World Report of Violence and Health* (Geneva: World Health Organization, 2002), 149.

2. Marie M. Fortune, *Is Nothing Sacred? The Story of a Pastor, the Women He Sexually Abused, and the Congregation He Nearly Destroyed* (San Francisco: Harper and Row, 1989), xiv.

3. L. Heise, M. Ellsberg, and M. Gottemoeller, *Ending Violence against Women*. Population Reports, Series L, no. 11 (Baltimore: Johns Hopkins University School of Public Health, December 1999), 2. http://www.infoforhealth.org/pr/l11/violence.pdf (accessed November 30, 2007).

4. *No to Violence* is a publication of the Male Family Violence Prevention Association, an Australian organization that works with men to assist them to change and to end their violent behavior. www.ntv.net.au.

5. Mary Anne Hildebrand, "Domestic Violence: A Challenge to Mennonite Faith and Peace Theology," *Conrad Grebel Review* 10, no. 1 (Winter 1992): 74.

6. *Kin-dom* is a feminist term used to refer to the reign or kingdom of God. I first came across this concept in Letty Russell's lectures during my first two years in the D.Min. program at San Francisco Theological Seminary. Ada María Isasi-Díaz has also used it in her book *Mujerista Theology* (66, 83). This term describes not what *is*, but rather our vision of what the church *is to be*. The teachings of Jesus say that his kin-dom is not of this world but is to have a different set of values. In a feminist reading of Jesus, it is understood that Jesus understood his task as intended equally for all, that everyone enjoys the same relationship with him, that prestige and power are not sought.

7. Ada María Isasi-Díaz, *Mujerista Theology* (Maryknoll, NY: Orbis Books, 1996), 65–66.

8. Ibid., 74.

9. I, too, have painful stories of married Christian men, leaders in the church, inviting me to become sexually involved with them. I have written both in Spanish

and English about cases I have also dealt with, situations in which victims, both adolescent and adult women, have been abused by pastors in the United States.

10. J. Denny Weaver, *The Nonviolent Atonement* (Grand Rapids, MI: Eerdmans, 2000), 8–9. Weaver uses Walter Wink's convincing term, although his thesis proposes a new *Christus Victor*, in which he claims the rejection of violence is intrinsic to the narrative of Jesus. As a Mennonite theologian, Weaver focuses on Jesus' life and not on his violent death.

11. Susan Brooks Thistlethwaite, "Institutionalized Violence," in *Dictionary of Feminist Theologies*, ed. Letty M. Russell and J. Shannon Clarkson (Louisville, KY: Westminster/John Knox Press, 1996), 307.

12. Ruth Krall, email exchange with Dr. Krall in her role as an advisory professor during preparation of my doctoral dissertation.

13. Patricia Evans, *The Verbally Abusive Relationship: How to Recognize It and How to Respond* (Holbrook, MA: Adams Media Corporation, 1996), 15.

14. Hélder Câmara, *Spiral of Violence*, trans. Della Couling (London: Sheed and Ward, 1971), 41.

15. Ibid., 55.

16. Ibid., 56, 58.

17. John Paul Lederach, *Enredos, pleitos y problemas* (Guatemala City: Ediciones CLARA-SEMILLA, 1992), 7.

18. John Dear, *The God of Peace: Toward a Theology of Nonviolence* (Maryknoll, N.Y.: Orbis Books, 1994), 135.

19. Darla Schumm, "Violence Reconsidered: Mennonites, Patriarchy, and Violence" (master's thesis, Pacific School of Religion, 1992), 32.

20. Elizabeth Janeway, *Power of the Weak* (New York: Morrow Quill Paperbacks, 1980).

21. Pam McAllister, ed., *Reweaving the Web of Life: Feminism and Nonviolence* (Philadelphia: New Society Publishers, 1983), 28–29.

22. Dear, *The God of Peace*, 135.

23. U.S. Department of Justice, Office of Justice Program, "Family Violence Statistics" (June 2005), 4.

24. Richard J. Gelles and Donileen R. Loseke, eds., *Current Controversies on Family Violence* (Newbury Park, CA: Sage Publications, 1993), xi.

25. www. Rainbow-House.Org/WhatisDV.html.

26. http://www.ntv.net.au/index.html.

27. Olga Grau Duhart, "Familia: un grito de fin de siglo," *Revista Isis Internacional Ediciones de la Mujer* 20 (1994): 43–58.

28. Elsa Tamez, *Struggles for Power in Early Christianity* (Maryknoll, NY: Orbis Books, 2007), 27–28.

29. Grau Duhart, "Familia," 57.

30. Teresa J. Rothausen-Vange, "Family Diversity," in *Work-Family Encyclopedia*, ed. Stephen Sweet and Judi Casey (Boston: Sloan Work and Family Research Network, Boston College, April 2005). wfnet.bc.edu.

31. Ibid.

32. Amparo de Medina, *Libres de la violencia familiar* (El Paso, TX: Mundo Hispano, 2001), 25.

33. Ibid., 25.

34. Jorge Corsi, "Violencia familiar: Una mirada interdisciplinaria sobre un grave problema social," in *Sentir, Pensar y Enfrentar la Violencia Intrafamiliar: Lecturas complementarias*, ed. Ana Hidalgo (San José, Costa Rica: Instituto Nacional de las Mujeres Costa Rica, 1999), 211.

35. Medina, *Libres de la violencia familiar*, 29.

36. This is my way of classifying Christian churches that worship the Holy Spirit and see all reality through that lens. In these churches even scripture is often greatly spiritualized.

37. Just-war theory (in Latin, *jus ad bellum*) has become one way in which Christians have justified the use of war or violence. Just-war theory was first summarized by Thomas Aquinas and later adopted by the Reformers. Force was to be employed by sovereign political authorities and within the interpretation of Romans 13:1–6. The three main criteria to justify using force were to defend against attack, to retake something wrongly taken, and to punish evil. Anabaptist theology introduced another way for Christians to respond—by pacifism.

38. John R. Burkholder, "Can We Make Sense of Mennonite Peace Theology?" in *Mennonite Peace Theology: A Panorama of Types*, ed. John R. Burkholder and Barbara Nelson Gingerich (Akron, PA: Mennonite Central Committee, 1991), 7.

39. Ibid., 9.

40. Juan Driver, *Contra corriente: Ensayos sobre eclesiología radical* (Guatemala City: Ediciones CLARA-SEMILLA, 1988), 7.

41. Ibid., 11.

42. John Driver, *Images of the Church in Mission* (Scottdale, PA: Herald Press, 1997), 94.

43. *Ocho de marzo: Día Internacional de la Mujer* (Organización Femenina Popular de Barrancabermeja-Magdalena Medio-Bogotá for International Women's Day, March 8, 2002), 31.

44. James Newton Poling, *The Abuse of Power: A Theological Problem* (Nashville, TN: Abingdon Press, 1991), 17. Although Poling refers in his book exclusively to victims of abuse, I feel the discussion can readily apply to those suffering from family violence.

45. National Network for Family Resiliency, "Family Resiliency: Building Strengths to Meet Life's Challenges" (1993). www.clemson.edu/fyd/resiliency.htm.

46. Poling, *The Abuse of Power*, 180.

47. Schumm, "Violence Reconsidered," 35.

48. Ibid., 172–73.

49. This is particularly important for churches in developing countries where other counseling resources are often not available.

50. Poling, *The Abuse of Power*, 21.

51. The term *God-Sophia* or *Christ-Sophia* is often used by feminist theologians to highlight the feminine part of the Creator and to counter the image of God as male. Sophia is wisdom and represents the essence of God in motion.

2. Branches That Connect

1. While Jessica and Carmen have given permission for their stories to be shared, their names have been changed to protect their identity.

2. This document was prepared in response to the question, Is violence inherited? For the text, see www.unesco.org/shs/human rights/hrfv.htm (accessed June 27, 2007).

3. Elsa Tamez, "Cultural Violence against Women in Latin America," in *Women Resisting Violence: Spirituality for Life*, ed. Mary John Mananzan et al. (Maryknoll, NY: Orbis Books, 1996), 18.

4. Gioconda Batres Méndez, *El lado oculto de la masculinidad: Tratamiento para ofensores* (San José, Costa Rica: Programa Regional de la Capacitación Contra la Violencia Domestica, 1999), 12.

5. Ibid., 60.

6. Jorge Corsi, "Violencia familiar: Una mirada interdisciplinaria sobre un grave problema social," in *Sentir, Pensar y Enfrentar la Violencia Intrafamiliar*, ed. Ana Hildalgo (San José, Costa Rica: Instituto Nacional de las Mujeres, 1999), 50.

7. "Interview with Jorge Corsi during His Visit to El Salvador in 2004," in *Vertice.* www.elsalvador.com/vertice/2004/150804/entrevista.html (accessed September 2, 2007).

8. Corsi, "Violencia familiar," 14–15.

9. Maria Cristina Palacios Valencia, "La familia como ámbito de vida social: Escenario de encuentros y desencuentros," paper presented at the second training session on intra-family violence, Manizales, Colombia, November 1996.

10. Ibid., 16–17.

11. Ibid., 19.

12. Ibid., 20–21.

13. Quoted in Staff of Volcano Press, *Family Violence and Religion: An Interfaith Resource Guide* (Volcano, CA: Volcano Press, 1995), 252–54.

14. Ibid., 254.

15. Álvaro A. Fernández Gallego et al., *La Reconstrucción del Quindío* (Armenia, Colombia: Universidad del Quindío, 2002), 192–93.

16. Angela Maria Quintero Vásquez, "Nuevas perspectivas en el abordaje de la violencia intrafamiliar," *II Jornada de Capacitación sobre violencia familiar* [Manizales, Caldas: Secretaria de Salud de Manizales], ed. Lucia Franco Giraldo, Ana Maria Ocampo, and Rubén Cuartas Restrepo (November 1996): 12.

17. Etienne G. Krug et al., eds., *World Report on Violence and Health* (Geneva: WHO, 2002), 44. www.who.int/violence_injury_prevention/violence/world_report/en/full_en.pdf (accessed August 31, 2007).

18. Gallego et al., *La Reconstrucción del Quindío*, 210.

19. National Council on Child Abuse and Family Violence, "Should Children Exposed to Family Violence Be Considered Maltreated?" (June 4, 2007), 1. www.family violence.org/childrenfamily.htm (accessed August 30, 2007).

20. Amnesty International, "Worldwide Scandal: Poverty and Violence, a Vicious Cycle." www.amnesty.org/actforwomen/scandal-6-eng (accessed August 31, 2007).

21. National Organization for Women, "Violence Against Women in the United States," 1992. Available at www.now.org/issues/violence/stats.html (accessed August 31, 2007).

22. P. O'Campo et al., "Violence by Male Partners against Women during the Childbearing Years: A Contextual Analysis," *American Journal of Public Health* 85, no. 8 (1995): 1092–97.

23. "Sexual Violence," chapter 6 in Krug et al., *World Report on Violence and Health*, 150, 153–55.

24. National Sexual Violence Resource Center, *Unspoken Crimes: Sexual Assault in Rural America* (Enola, PA: National Sexual Violence Resource Center, 2003), 7.

25. Ibid., 21

26. Joint Center for Housing Studies of Harvard University, "Housing Challenges," *The State of the Nation's Housing 2007* (Cambridge, MA: Joint Center for Housing Studies of Harvard University, 2007), 25–30.

27. Amy K. Glasmeier, "The Nation We've Become," Poverty in America website (February 26, 2007). www.povertyinamerica.psu.edu/ (accessed on August 31, 2007).

28. Substance Abuse Treatment and Domestic Violence Series 25. www.ncadi.samhsa.gov/govpubs/bkd239/25f.aspx (accessed November 2, 2007).

29. National Center for PTSD, Department of Veterans Affairs, "Fact Sheet." www.ncptsd.va.gov/ (accessed September 3, 2007); "Veterans Report Mental Distress," *Washington Post* (March 1, 2006).

30. Molly Butler Bailey, "Improving the Sentencing of Domestic Violence Offenders in Maine: A Proposal to Prohibit Anger Management Therapy," *Maine Bar Journal* (Summer 2006), 141; available online.

31. Walter Riso, *Intimidades masculinas* (Bogotá: Editorial Norma, 1998), 178, 180–81.

32. Lorraine Bernis, Phyllis Drennan-Searson and Vern Redekop, eds., *Family Violence in a Patriarchal Culture: A Challenge to Our Way of Living* (Ottowa: The Keith Press, 1988), 41.

33. In Carol J. Adams and Marie M. Fortune, eds., *Violence against Women and Children* (New York: Continuum Publishing, 1998), 456.

34. Batres Méndez, *El lado oculto de la masculinidad*, 60.

35. Florence Thomas, who is French, has been living in Bogotá, Colombia, for over two decades. She has been instrumental in creating space within the Universidad Nacional of Bogotá for discussions on gender analysis and women's rights. She has used this phrase in many presentations.

36. Elizabeth Janeway, *Power of the Weak* (New York: Morrow Quill Paperbacks, 1980), 100.

37. Bernis, Drennan-Serason, and Redekop, *Family Violence in a Patriarchal Culture*, 13.

38. See the Federal Child Abuse Prevention and Treatment Act (42 USCA §5106g) and Public Law 108–36, June 25, 2003; available online.

39. Detailed reports and statistics are available online. See, for example, www.acf.hhs.gov/programs/cb/pubs/cm05/index.htm and www.childwelfare.gov/can/prevalence/stats (accessed November 1, 2007).

40. Bruce Harris, "State Violence against Children," presentation of Casa Alianza/Covenant House Latin America to the United Nations' Committee on the Rights of the Child, Geneva, September 22, 2000. www.crin.org/docs/resources/treaties/crc.25/casaalia.pdf (accessed December 15, 2007).

41. Miriam K. Ehrensaft, Patricia Cohen, and Jocelyn Brown, "Intergenerational Transmission of Partner Violence: A 20–Year Prospective Study," *Journal of Counseling and Clinical Psychology* 71, no. 4 (2003): 741–53. www.apa.org/journals/releases/ccp714741.pdf (accessed September 3, 2007).

42. Child Welfare Information Gateway, "Long-Term Consequences of Child Abuse and Neglect Factsheet" (2006). www.childwelfare.gov/pubs/factsheet/long_term_consequences.cfm (accessed November 2, 2007).

43. Quintero Vásquez, "Nuevas perspectivas en el abordaje de la violencia intrafamiliar," 22.

44. Maria Cristina Salazar and Peter Oakley, *Niños y violencia: El caso de América Latina* (Bogotá: Editorial Tercer Mundo, 1993), 52.

45. Freddy Arango, "El sexo se compra en 'La Libertad,'" *El Tiempo* (February 23, 2003).

46. Mike Earl-Taylor, "HIV/AIDS, the Stats, the Virgin Cure, and Infant Rape," *Science in Africa: Africa's First On-Line Science Magazine* (April 2002). www.scienceinafrica.co.za (accessed November 2, 2007).

47. Donald H. Dunson, *No Room at the Table: Earth's Most Vulnerable Children* (Maryknoll, NY: Orbis Books, 2003); see also various reports from UNICEF, UNESCO, International Save the Children Alliance, and Defence for Children International.

48. Salazar and Oakley, *Niños y violencia*, 185–86.

49. Ibid., 17.

50. Janeway, *The Power of the Weak*, 11.

51. Melissa A. Miller, *Family Violence: The Compassionate Church Responds* (Scottdale, PA: Herald Press, 1994), 21.

52. Ibid., chaps. 1–4.

53. Corsi, "Violencia familiar," 20–27.

54. Ibid., 26.

55. Krug et al., *World Report on Violence and Health*, 12–13.

56. Quintero Vásquez, "Nuevas perspectivas en el abordaje de la violencia intrafamiliar,"14.

57. For current statistics on the wage gap, see, for example, www. pay-equity.org/info and www.maineaflcio.org/womenequalpay.

58. Corsi, "Violencia familiar," 27.

59. David Grossman, *On Killing: The Psychological Cost of Learning to Kill in War and Society* (Boston: Little, Brown, and Company, 1996), xviii.

60. Batres Méndez, *El lado oculto de la masculinidad*, 11.

61. Amy Holtzworth-Monroe and Gregory Stuart, "Testing of Male Batterers Typology," *Journal of Consultation and Clinical Psychology* 68, no. 6 (1994): 1000–1019.

62. Batres Méndez, *El lado oculto de la masculinidad*, 61.

63. Walter Riso, *Intimidades masculinas* (Bogotá: Editorial Norma, 1998).

64. Robert Moore and Douglas Gillette, *King, Warrior, Magician, Lover: Rediscovering the Archetypes of the Mature Masculine* (San Francisco: Harper San Francisco, 1990).

65. Oswaldo Montoya Tèlleria, *Nadando contra corriente* (Managua: Punto de Encuentro, 1998), 27–37.

66. Ibid., 93.

67. Ibid., 109.

68. The MCC is the agency of the Mennonite churches in the USA and Canada that works on development and social justice.

69. Carolyn Holderread Heggen, presentation at Working Together as a Peace Church Committed to Preventing Family Violence, sponsored by the MCC, Akron, Pennyslvania, May 18–20, 2001. Available in Spanish from the MCC.

70. Irving Pérez, "Análisis social de los factores culturales que facilitan el problema de violencia familiar," presentation at Working Together as a Peace Church Committed to Preventing Family Violence, sponsored by the MCC, Akron, Pennyslvania, May 18–20, 2001.

71. Thomas Songer, *The Epidemiology of Domestic Violence* (Pittsburgh: University of Pittsburgh, Center for Injury Research and Control, 2005. www.pitt.edu/~epi2670/domestic/domestic%20violence.pdf.

72. Pérez, "Análisis social de los factores culturales que facilitan el problema de violencia familiar."

73. For more information about Bridge of Hope, and about how to start additional branches, see www.bridgeofhope.org.

3. Nutrients within the Trunk

1. Howard John Loewen, *One Lord, One Church, One Hope, and One God* (Elkhart, IN: Institute of Mennonite Studies, 1985), 79–82; Guy F. Hershberger, *War, Peace, and Nonresistance* (Scottdale, PA: Herald Press, 1969), 97–98.

2. In 1660 T. J. van Bragt published the oldest documents about the Dutch martyrs titled *Martyrs Mirror*, still well known today among the Mennonites (Thieleman van Bragt, *Martyrs Mirror: The Story of Fifteen Centuries of Christian Martyrdom from the Time of Christ to A.D. 1660*, trans. Joseph F. Sohm, 2nd ed. [Scottdale, PA: Herald Press, 2001]).

3. Guy Franklin Hershberger, "Nonresistance," in *The Mennonite Encyclopedia* (Scottdale, PA: Herald Press, 1957), 898.

4. C. Arnold Snyder, "Reflections on Mennonite Uses of Anabaptist History," in *Mennonite Peace Theology: A Panorama of Types*, ed. John Richard Burkholder and Barbara Nelson Gingerich (Akron, PA: MCC, 1991), 85–86.

5. Guy Franklin Hershberger's main argument is precisely the concept of nonresistance, which in his understanding moves away from confronting the evildoer and provoking more violence. See Guy Franklin Hershberger, *War, Peace, and Nonresistance: A Classic Statement of a Mennonite Peace Position in Faith and Practice* (Scottdale, PA: Herald Press, 1991 <1953>), 97ff.

6. Ibid., 101.
7. Ibid., 98.
8. Ibid., 102–3.
9. Ibid., 110, 113–14.
10. Harold S. Bender, "The Anabaptist Vision," *Mennonite Quarterly Review* 18 (April 1944): 67–88.
11. John C. Wenger, *Disciples of Jesus* (Scottdale, PA: Herald Press, 1977). The first copy, titled *Discipleship*, was released as a homemade booklet in the late 1950s; later Herald Press edited the material and published it as *Disciples of Jesus*.
12. Elizabeth Bauman, *Coals of Fire*, illus. Allan Eitzen (Scottdale, PA: Herald Press, 1954).
13. Hershberger, *War, Peace, and Nonresistance*, 147–48, 150–53.
14. Beulah Stauffer Hostetler, "Nonresistance and Social Responsibility: Mennonites and Mainline Peace Emphasis, ca. 1950 to 1958," *The Mennonite Quarterly Review* 64 (1990): 49–73.
15. Hershberger, *War, Peace, and Nonresistance*, 173.
16. Hostetler, "Nonresistance and Social Responsibility," 58.
17. Ibid., 70.
18. Darla Schumm, "Nonviolence Reconsidered: Mennonite, Patriarchy and Violence" (master's thesis, Pacific School of Religion, 1992), 31.
19. John Richard Burkholder and Barbara Nelson Gingerich, eds., *Mennonite Peace Theology: A Panorama of Types* (Akron, PA: MCC, 1991). 10. The Schleitheim Confession written in 1527 was the first confession of faith done by Anabaptist groups in the Swiss area.
20. An extreme example of this withdrawal is the lifestyle of the Amish, "cousins" of the Mennonites.
21. Robert Friedmann, *The Theology of the Anabaptists* (Scottdale, PA: Herald Press, 1973), 43–45.
22. Janneken L. Smucker, "A Curriculum of One's Own: The Emergence of the Women's Studies Program at Goshen College" (Goshen, IN: Mennonite Historical Library, December 8, 1997).
23. Elizabeth G. Yoder, ed., *Peace Theology and Violence against Women* (Elkhart, IN: Institute of Mennonite Studies, 1992), iii–iv. This consultation served to strengthen the community peace church as it was working on violence against women and peace theology, as Yoder mentions in the preface.
24. On occasion, other evangelical churches have accused the Mennonite Church of being more interested in humanitarian work than in spreading the gospel.
25. In Latin America this is known as *teología del camino*, a concept shared by Anabaptist and liberation theologians. This is a good example of a theological concept shaped by the times; it is as valid today as it was in the sixteenth century, although its applications are somewhat different.
26. Richard B. Gregg, *The Power of Nonviolence*, 2nd ed. (New York: Schocken Books, 1959 <1934>), 72.
27. Sharon H. Ringe, "When Women Interpret the Bible," in *The Women's Bible Commentary*, ed. Carol A. Newsom and Sharon H. Ringe (Louisville, KY: Westminster/John Knox Press, 1992), 3.

28. First advanced by scripture scholar Elisabeth Schüssler Fiorenza in 1992, a short description may be found in Amy-Jill Levine, "Hermeneutics of Suspicion," in *Dictionary of Feminist Theologies*, ed. Letty M. Russell and J. Shannon Clarkson (Louisville, KY: Westminster/John Knox Press, 1996), 140–41. Feminist scholars understand that biblical texts, written by men, are the product of a patriarchal way of seeing the world.

29. Walter Wink, *Engaging the Powers: Discernment and Resistance in a World of Domination* (Minneapolis: Fortress Press, 1992), 175–76.

30. Richard Gardner, *Matthew*, Believers Church Bible Commentary (Scottdale, PA: Herald Press, 1991), 109.

31. Wink, *Engaging the Powers*, 176, 185.

32. Ibid., 176.

33. Ibid.

34. Warren Carter, *Matthew and the Margins: A Sociopolitical and Religious Reading* (Maryknoll, NY: Orbis Books, 2000), 151.

35. Ibid., 152.

36. Ibid.

37. Juan Driver, *Contra corriente: Ensayos sobre eclesiología radical* (Guatemala City: Ediciones CLARA-SEMILLA, 1998), 6.

38. Gardner, *Matthew*, 111.

39. Driver, *Contra corriente*, 7.

40. Dionisio Byler, *Jesus y la no Violencia* (Bogotá: Ediciones CLARA, 1993), 88.

41. This quotation appears in Spanish on a poster at the Episcopal Office in Guatemala City (April 24, 2003).

42. Gardner, *Matthew*, 113.

43. Menno Simons, in *The Complete Writings of Menno Simons* (Scottdale, PA: Herald Press, 1956), 551.

44. Joanne Carlson Brown and Rebecca Parker, "For God So Loved the World?" in *Christianity, Patriarchy, and Abuse: A Feminist Critique*, ed. Joanne Carlson Brown and Carole R. Bohn (New York: Pilgrim Press, 1990), 2, 3.

45. *Womanist*, a term used by African American feminists, was first used by Alice Walker and later given theological meaning by black theologian Delores S. Williams.

46. J. Denny Weaver, *The Nonviolent Atonement* (Grand Rapids, MI: Eerdmans, 2001), 5.

47. This term was first used by Gustaf Aulén in his book *Christus Victor: An Historical Study of the Three Main Types of the Idea of Atonement*, trans. A. G. Herbert (New York: Macmillan, 1969).

48. Weaver, *The Nonviolent Atonement*, 175.

49. Rosemary Radford Ruether, *Women and Redemption: A Theological History* (Minneapolis: Fortress Press, 1998), 279.

50. Brown and Parker, "For God So Loved the World?" 27–28.

51. John Driver, *Understanding the Atonement for the Mission of the Church* (Scottdale, PA: Herald Press, 1986), 15–19.

52. Ibid., 19.

53. Ibid., 51.

54. Ibid., 29–30.

55. Weaver, *The Nonviolent Atonement*, 2.

56. René Girard, *The Scapegoat*, trans. Ivonne Freccero (Baltimore: Johns Hopkins University Press, 1986), 117.

57. Ibid.

58. Weaver, *The Nonviolent Atonement*, 49.

59. Sally B. Purvis, "Cross," in Russell and Clarkson, *Dictionary of Feminist Theologies*, 62.

60. Schumm, "Nonviolence Reconsidered," 88–89.

61. Flora A. Keshgegian, "Suffering," in Russell and Clarkson, *Dictionary of Feminist Theologies*, 279.

62. Dorothee Soelle, *Suffering* (Philadelphia: Fortress Press, 1975), 164.

63. Ibid., 5.

64. Ibid., 29.

65. Ibid., 108, 109.

66. Delores S. Williams, in Russell and Clarkson, *Dictionary of Feminist Theologies*, 280.

67. Dorothee Soelle, *The Silent Cry: Mysticism and Resistance* (Minneapolis: Fortress Press, 2001), 209.

68. Soelle, *Suffering*, 173.

69. Peter Stucky, Anabaptist theologian and pastor of the Colombian Mennonite Church, interview by author, June 19, 2003, Bogotá, Colombia. Peter is the son of the Mennonite couple sent to start mission work in Colombia in 1947. He was born and raised in Colombia and considers himself very much a Latin American with Mennonite North American roots.

70. Driver, *Contra corriente*, xi–xiv.

71. Ibid., xvi.

72. Ibid., xv–xvi, xvii.

73. Ibid., xvi.

74. Stucky, personal interview.

75. Letty M. Russell, "Ecclesiology," in Russell and Clarkson, *Dictionary of Feminist Theologies*, 75–76.

76. Elsa Tamez, "An Ecclesial Community: Women's Vision and Voices," *The Ecumenical Review* (January 2001): 62.

77. Ibid., 61, 62.

78. Letty M. Russell, "Hot-House Ecclesiology: A Feminist Interpretation of the Church," *The Ecumenical Review* (January 2001): 49.

79. I have written in Spanish using words beginning with "s" (*salvacion*—healing, *santidad*—holy, *sanidad*—healing), demonstrating they are all part of *shalom*, meaning peace or well-being.

80. Driver, *Contra corriente*, 84.

81. Ibid.

82. Although he wanted to share his story publicly at the gathering, I have changed his name to maintain his privacy.

4. Exposing the Roots

1. Mary Ellsberg, in Claudia Garcia-Moreno et al., "More Than a Social Problem," *Science* 310 (2005): 1282–83.

2. *The American Heritage Dictionary of the English Language*, ed. William Morris (Boston: Houghton Mifflin, 1976), 321.

3. C. Garcia-Moreno et al., "WHO Multi-Country Study on Women's Health and Domestic Violence against Women" (Seattle, WA: PATH/WHO, 2005). www.who.int/gender/violence/who_multicountry_study/en/index.html.

4. Samara L. Firebaugh, "Culture of Violence Does Desensitize," letter to the editor in response to Eric J. Plosky's column "Reflecting on Littleton, Colorado" after the school shootings, *The Tech Online Edition* 119, no. 24 (May 4, 1999). www-tech.mit.edu/V119/.

5. "A Culture of Violence: Gender of School Shooters Leaves Questions," *The Daily Tarheel* (September 5, 2006). www.dailytarheel.com.

6. *Walking Together*, Samaritan Counseling Center newsletter (November 2006).

7. Joanna Dewey, "The Gospel of Mark," in *Searching the Scriptures: A Feminist Commentary*, ed. Elisabeth Schüssler Fiorenza (New York: Crossroad, 1994), 490–91.

8. Fernando Belo, *A Materialist Reading of the Gospel of Mark* (Maryknoll, NY: Orbis Books, 1981), 167–68..

9. Ibid., 168.

10. Dewey, "The Gospel of Mark," 491.

11. Ched Myers et al., *"Say to This Mountain": Mark's Story of Discipleship* (Maryknoll, NY: Orbis Books, 1996), 118, 117.

12. Carolyn Holderread Heggen, *Sexual Abuse in Christian Homes and Churches* (Scottdale, PA: Herald Press, 1993), 126, 125.

13. As part of a treatment and restoration process, we recommend that an abuser stay away from the community until the healing of both the community and the person has taken place, in order to create a safe place within the community, particularly for the victim.

14. See Denise M. Ackerman, "Power," in *Dictionary of Feminist Theologies*, ed. Letty M. Russell and J. Shannon Clarkson (Louisville, KY: Westminster/John Knox Press, 1996), 221.

15. Dewey, "The Gospel of Mark," 493.

16. Myers et al., *"Say to This Mountain,"* 116, 118.

17. Janice Love, "The Decade to Overcome Violence: Harvest from an Ecumenical Journey," *The Ecumenical Review* 53, no. 2 (April 2002): 145.

18. The curriculum was part of my research project for a doctor of ministry degree under the auspices of the International Feminist Program of the San Francisco Theological Seminary in 2002. The curriculum was implemented during my service in Colombia.

19. James Newton Poling, *The Abuse of Power: A Theological Problem* (Nashville, TN: Abingdon Press, 1991), 27–29, 179.

20. Paulo Freire, *Pedagogy of the Oppressed* (New York: Continuum, 1970), chap. 1. First published in Portuguese in 1967.

21. Maria Cristina Palacios Valencia, "La familia como ámbito de vida social: Escenario de encuentros y desencuentros," paper presented at the second training session on intra-family violence, Manizales, Colombia, November 1996.

22. Olga Grau Duhart, "Familia: un grito de fin de siglo," *Revista Isis Internacional*, Ediciones de la Mujer 20 (1994): 44.

23. Center for the Prevention of Sexual and Domestic Violence, *Broken Promises*, video (Seattle, WA, 1999).

24. An experienced colleague once reminded me, "If you think you are in control of your child, think again; it's only an illusion." I have used this expression many times in parenting classes I teach through the Church of the Brethren Youth Services.

25. UNICEF, "Women: Progress and Disparity" (1997). www.unicef.org/pon97/p48a.htm.

26. See *The Legal Status of Rural Women in Nineteen Latin America Countries* (Rome: Food and Agriculture Organization of the United Nations, 1994). www.fao.org/docrep/.

27. Shankar Vedantam, "Harm Outweighs Benefits of Spanking," *Washington Post* (June 26, 2002).

28. Jim Fay and Foster W. Cline, *The Love and Logic Journal* (Golden, CO: The Love and Logic Press, 1995).

29. Frank Albrecht, "Raising the Odds for Having Responsible Children through Disciplining with Love and Logic," *The Mennonite* (May 6, 2003), 11.

30. Ibid., 12–13.

31. Frank Albrecht, "Rituals That Form Character." Used with permission of the author.

32. Salvador Minuchin with Michael P. Nichols, *Family Healing: Strategies for Hope and Understanding* (New York: The Free Press, 1998), 177.

33. Michael P. Nichols, *The Power of Family Therapy* (New York: Fireside, Simon and Schuster, 1988), 205–6.

34. Minuchin and Nichols, *Family Healing*, 230, 234.

35. Ibid., 196–200.

36. Marie J. Giblin, "Hierarchy," in Russell and Clarkson, *Dictionary of Feminist Theologies*, 143.

37. Olga Lucía López Jaramillo, "Terapia sistémica y la violencia conyugal como motivo de consulta," paper presented at the second training session on intra-family violence, Manizales, Colombia, October 1996.

38. Ruth Krall, e-mail exchange on a feminist reading on family therapy. Used with permission.

39. Virginia Satir, *The New Peoplemaking* (Mountain View, CA: Science and Behavior Books, 1988), 27. See also Virginia Satir and Michele Baldwin, *Satir Step by Step: A Guide to Creating Change in Families* (Palo Alto, CA: Science and Behavior Books, 1983), 206–22.

40. Salvador Minuchin, *Families and Family Therapy* (Cambridge, MA: Harvard University Press, 1974), 256.

41. This follows the three stops outlined by Minuchin (see ibid., 119).
42. Based on the Institute for Peace and Justice, "Family Pledge of Nonviolence" (St. Louis, MO), loose leaf.
43. Freire, *Pedagogy of the Oppressed*, chap. 1.
44. Jennifer Atlee-Loudon, *Red Thread: A Spiritual Journal of Accompaniment, Trauma, and Healing* (Washington, DC: Ecumenical Program in Central America and the Caribbean, 2001), 17.
45. Ibid., 145.

5. Peace That Brings Healing

1. United States Conference of Catholic Bishops, "Confronting a Culture of Violence: A Catholic Framework for Action" (Washington, DC: USCCB, 1994).
2. United Nations Resolution A/RES/53/243, Declaration and Program of Action on a Culture of Peace; and Resolution A/RES/52/13, Culture of Peace.
3. www.ifuw.org.
4. See, for example, Birgit Brock-Utne, *Educating for Peace: A Feminist Perspective* (Oxford: Pergamon, 1985); and idem, *Feminist Perspectives on Peace and Peace Education* (Burlington, MA: Elsevier, 1989).
5. See Mary John Manazan et al., eds., *Women Resisting Violence: Spirituality for Life* (Maryknoll, NY: Orbis Books, 1996), 23–25.
6. Elise Boulding, *Cultures of Peace: The Hidden Side of History* (Syracuse, NY: Syracuse University Press, 2000).
7. See Ivone Gebara, *Longing for Running Water: Biblical Reflections on Ministry* (Minneapolis: Fortress Press, 1999); and idem, *Out of the Depths: Women's Experience of Evil and Salvation* (Minneapolis: Fortress Press, 2002). See also Rosemary Radford Ruether, *Gaia and God: An Ecofeminist Theology of Earth Healing* (San Francisco: HarperSanFrancisco, 1992).
8. Mary Ellsberg and Lori Heise, *Researching Violence against Women: A Practical Guide for Researchers and Activists* (New York: WHO, 2005), 5. This comprehensive report, a joint publication of PATH and WHO, and a summary of it, are also available on the website of PATH, "an international, nonprofit organization that works worldwide to break longstanding cycles of poor health" (www.PATH.org).
9. C. Garcia-Moreno et al., "WHO Multi-Country Study on Women's Health and Domestic Violence against Women" (Seattle, WA: PATH/WHO, 2005), 22–27. www.who.int/gender/violence/who_multicountry_study/en/index.html.
10. The complete texts of UN documents are available on the Internet.
11. See Roger J. R. Levesque, *Culture and Family Violence: Fostering Change through Human Rights Law* (Washington, DC: American Psychological Association, 2001), 6, 85.
12. Ibid., 154.
13. Ibid., 39–40.

14. Michael L. Penn and Rahel Nardos, *Overcoming Violence against Women and Girls: The International Campaign to Eradicate a Worldwide Problem* (Lanham, MD: Rowman and Littlefield Publishers, 2003), 110–11.

15. Albert J. Reiss, Jr., and Jeffrey A. Roth, eds., *Understanding and Preventing Violence* (Washington, DC: National Academy Press, 1993), 21.

16. Murray A. Straus, Richard J. Gelles, and Suzanne K. Steinmetz, *Behind Closed Doors: Violence in the American Family* (New York: Anchor Press, 1980), 237–44.

17. Richard J. Gelles, *Intimate Violence in Families* (Thousand Oaks, CA: Sage Publications, 1990), 183–85, 194.

18. Ben Silliman, "Resilient Families: Qualities of Families Who Survive and Thrive," University of Wyoming Cooperative Extension Service, B-1018 (June 1995). ces.uwyo.edu/PUBS/WY1018.PDF.

19. Marie Fortune, *Is Nothing Sacred? The Story of a Pastor, the Women He Sexually Abused, and the Congregation He Nearly Destroyed* (San Francisco: Harper and Row, 1989).

20. USCCB, "Confronting a Culture of Violence."

21. John Paul II, "Urbi et Orbi Message" (Christmas 2000), nos. 4–5. www.vatican.va/holy_father/john_paul_ii/messages/urbi/documents/hf_jp-ii_mes_20001225_urbi_en.html.

22. www.mcc.org/manitoba/vnv/.

23. Ruth E. Krall, "War and Family Violence: Women and Children Reap the Whirlwind," paper presented at a meeting organized by New Call to Peacemaking, Peacemaking in the Nuclear Family, August 1995, Richmond, Indiana, 10.

24. Charlotte S. Kasl, *Many Paths, One Journey: Moving Beyond the 12 Steps* (New York: Harper, 1992), Introduction. For a complete description of Dr. Kasl's program, see www.charlottekasl.com.

25. Garcia-Moreno et al., "WHO Multi-Country Study on Women's Health and Domestic Violence against Women," Preface.

26. Madeleine L'Engle, "Foreword," in Johann Christoph Arnold, *Seeking Peace* (Farmington, PA: Plough Publishing, 1998), xi.

27. Arnold, *Seeking Peace*, 23.

28. Ibid.

29. Albert Einstein, address, California Institute of Technology, February 16, 1931. www.salsa.net/peace/conv/8weekconv6-4.html (accessed November 6, 2007).

30. Alan Kreider, Eleanor Kreider, and Paulus Widjaja, *A Culture of Peace: God's Vision for the Church* (Intercourse, PA: Good Books, 2005), 35.

31. Ibid., 108.

32. Shirin Shokouhi, *Mandating America to Treatment: A Counselor's Perspective*. www.commondreams.org/views07/march2007.htm (accessed November 9, 2007).

33. Melissa Miller, *Family Violence: The Compassionate Church Responds* (Scottdale, PA: Herald Press, 1994), 147.

34. J. Lawrence Burkholder, "Nonresistance, Nonviolent Resistance, and Power," in *The Recovery of the Anabaptist*, ed. Guy F. Hershberger (Scottdale, PA: Herald Press, 1957), 135.

35. These are private stories women have shared with me. I admire their re-sourcefulness. Most of them had the support of their adult children and a long history of living in an abusive relationship. While these were the choices of my friends, and I respect that, in no way do I promote this option.

36. "Final Statement of the 'Women against Violence' Dialogue," in Manazan et al., *Women Resisting Violence*, 182–84.

37. Ibid., 184.

38. Krall, "War and Family Violence, 10.

Index